REFLECTIONS

By

GARY W. DICKINSON

This is the true story of my search for peace and personal growth, while living my dream of sailing the Pacific Coast alone in the boat I built.

INKWATER PRESS

PORTLAND • OREGON

INKWATERPRESS.COM

Cover and interior design by Masha Shubin
Cover photo © Gary W. Dickinson *Pilgrim* anchored at Lost Slough in the Delta
Author photo by Ryan Lowe

www.inkwaterpress.com

ISBN-13 978-1-59299-365-9
ISBN-10 1-59299-365-6

Publisher: Inkwater Press

Printed in the U.S.A.
All paper is acid free and meets all ANSI standards for archival quality paper.

rev1

TABLE OF CONTENTS

ACKNOWLEDGMENTS

TO MY PARENTS, Robert and Mamie Dickinson, for giving me the freedom and courage to pursue my dreams. To my daughter Tashera Dickinson, who inspired me to record this adventure. To Barbara Hutton, who encouraged me to share this story with others. To Joel Garcia, whose feedback was enlightening. To my sister Debra Donzella, whose encouragement helped to bring out my best. To my brothers Bob and Craig Dickinson, whose faith in me helped me finish what I started. To my only son Timothy Dickinson, with whom I have had the privilege of sharing more adventures than I can recall. To Rose Dickinson, who has shared more than twenty-five years of adventures and misadventures with me, and to the fine staff at Inkwater Press, who helped bring this book to be published. Thank you all. Without each of your lives touching mine this would not have been possible.

PREFACE

WORDS CAN BE a window to the writer's soul, and you can learn a lot about someone by reading their words. Being separated from my daughter, I hoped that she could get to know me by reading my account of the adventure I was about to begin. The worst thing about sailing alone is having no one to share the amazing discoveries with. Putting this story to paper would allow my daughter and other readers to share in the adventure with me.

This story is more of a quest than it is living out a childhood dream. I was searching for peace in the turmoil that was my life. At twenty-seven years of age my life was falling apart. I did not feel like I fit in or belonged.

The vehicle for this discovery was *Maranatha*, a twenty-six-foot wood sailboat that I built by hand.

During the six months of this voyage I discovered some secrets that forever changed me and my outlook on life. I found the peace I was longing for and realized that happiness is not measured by the things we acquire but by the lives we touch.

REFLECTIONS

1.
THE BEGINNING

AS I PREPARED to release the mooring lines that secured me to the life I had known, I began to reflect on the events that had brought me to this place. My life seemed like a series of beginnings and endings. Where should I start?

One of the first steps leading to this place began when I was nineteen years old. I had married my high school sweetheart and was looking forward to the challenges that life would bring to us. Regrettably one and a half years later I would be facing these challenges alone. There was an emptiness in my soul and I had to fill it with something. I had always dreamed of seeing the world, and a sailboat promised me the escape I was looking for.

With little research, and my only real experience working with wood having come from shop class in high school, I ordered blueprints for a twenty-six-foot center-cockpit sailboat that I would build from scratch. I would fill the emptiness in my life for the next two and one-half years by building this boat from a pile of lumber and one day fulfill my dream.

As time passed my broken heart began to mend and I thought

that I had found someone who would share my dream and the adventures that would surely follow. Once again I was wrong, and after two years, alone again.

I believe we are all connected. Each life we touch in turn touches the lives of others.

In the fall of 1980, two of my friends suddenly discovered that they had inoperable cancer and were not expected to live more than a few months. I remember a talk I had with one of them in the hospital. She kept telling me of the things she never had the chance to do. She said that when she got out of the hospital she would go to see St. Peter's Cathedral on the East Coast. She never got the chance to do that.

This incident was the grain of sand that finally tipped the scales that had started to tip years ago. I am determined not to live with regrets of what I have not done. I am not going to grow old saying I wish I had done this or that. This scale first started to tip with the death of my friend Ed Bert.

With love I remember his jokes and the part of himself that he gave to others. I remember sharing a common dream with him. We were building our boats at the same time. Mine a twenty-six-foot wood sailboat and Ed's a Cascade forty-two-foot sailboat. I finished my boat first, but then again, it is half the size of his. I remember the excitement in the talks that I had with Ed about where he was going to go when he launched his boat. Just to give you an idea of the type of person Ed was, the name of his vessel was going to be *Second Chance* and the name on his boat's dinghy would be *Last Chance*.

Ed's dream was born on a passage he made from Hawaii to Alaska. In spite of the odds against them making a safe passage, and the storms they encountered, they made it and his dream took root and grew during that trip. I am sure the expectation of fulfilling his dream gave him something to look forward to over the years. That is more than most people have.

Ed owned a refrigeration company, which he built from nothing to a successful company. After selling his business he was anxious to begin living out his dream. Ed filled out his retirement papers a few days before he and his wife Sue attended a retirement party for them at the Yacht Club. The day after that party Ed died.

I can think of no worse place to be in life than in the place of indecision. I have made my decision and I am willing to take the risk for my future. I can no longer sit on the fence deciding if I should sail away or not. Having made my choice, I now have to deal with the hundreds of things that need to be done to prepare for my voyage into the unknown.

I have known people who write themselves notes to remind them of things they have to do. I am generally not that type of person but the weeks before my departure I had notes to remind me of other notes. The lists seemed almost endless. Needed charts, supplies, spare parts, stores. I am sure anyone who has taken a long voyage before knows all too well the confusion that precedes an extended voyage. I had to get a power of attorney, set up automatic payments, etc.

I would always be asked the same two questions: Are you excited about going, and why are you going? To the first question I would answer no. You see, I have wanted to leave twice before. The first time was in 1975 but the boat was not finished, and again in 1976 when *Mary* was launched, but by that time I had remarried and the dream got lost in the shuffle. For these reasons I would not believe that I was actually going to leave until I cast off the mooring lines. Several people said that they envied me, but that is easy for someone to say. They did not make the sacrifices I have that brought me to this place I now find myself.

The reasons for this trip had changed for me. I was not going in search of adventure or even escape. The way my life had been going, above all else I was searching for peace. I knew that peace was not here or there but that it was within myself. I just needed time to sort things out and readjust my priorities. I had not been coping very well in several areas of my life, areas that I felt I had no control over. I was fighting and it was a fight I could not win. To say the least, the quality of my life was very poor.

Since the time I was in junior high school I had worked for a major grocery chain. For the previous ten years I got up every morning and went to work. I had worked my way up from a courtesy clerk or bagger to finishing the Store Management Training program, a prerequisite for becoming a Store Manager. I think you could say that I felt secure in my job and line of work. When I look back on the reasons that I went to work in the first place, they were not very different from those of the other kids my age, that being to buy a car. I think that we all have twenty-twenty hindsight, although many times I wish that I would have had twenty-twenty foresight. I feel like I never had the chance to be a teenager. It is very possible that I did not really miss a thing but I have always wondered.

I think that we all have a false sense of security that we place in the jobs we hold. Even though I knew that there really was not any, in the back of my mind I felt a sense of security. Maybe just the fact that things had continued as they had for the last ten years or more had a great deal to do with that feeling.

Originally I was going to take a leave of absence from my job, but two weeks before I was to leave I was told that I would have to quit and that I could be rehired when I returned from the trip. My past dealings with the company told me that their word meant nothing unless it was written down and then only because they would not want to look bad in the eyes of the public. Since I did not have anything on paper from the company I did not put much faith in their promise. I think that in most big corporations the employees are just another commodity to be used as the company sees fit.

Knowing all this I still felt scared at the thought of giving up not only my job but my entire lifestyle as I know it, friends, family, and all of the things that gave me a feeling of belonging. The changes that I would be going through and the fear of what might be in store for me gave me a lot to think about.

This is one of those times that I thought, if I did not take the chance now I might never get another one. Whether it would be a good choice or not I did not know, but I would rather take the chance of losing than to always wonder, what if?

I had learned an expensive lesson several months before that you cannot put much importance on material things. I came home from work one day to find my house empty. Everything I had valued was gone and all that was left was an empty shell. When this happened to me it completed a change in my thinking that started some time earlier. The Bible says that "where your treasure is there will your heart be also." The important things in life to me became the things that would last forever. The love of family and friends and the memories I have that make me who I am. The things I value now no one can ever take from me. That is real security!

I place a good deal of weight in feelings and I had a feeling from the start that this trip was something that I would have to do alone. I am very grateful for the knowledge and companionship that I received from Curt Nielsen, who began this leg of the voyage with me.

Maranatha was the name I chose for my sailboat. I called her *Mary* for short. I chose this name for several reasons. My faith is the main reason for choosing this name. The definition is, O Lord come (Webster's Encyclopedic Unabridged Dictionary). The second reason I chose this name is because it is said that the more vowels in the name of the vessel, the more luck you will have with the boat. I figured that I needed all the luck I could get. *Mary* was a lot heavier when I finally left on the adventure than she was designed for. Instead of a medium displacement cruiser she became a heavy displacement one. I painted the water line four inches higher and with all the stuff I had on board she was now riding on that raised water line. When I think back on the amount of supplies and spare parts I crammed into a twenty-six by eight foot space, I can hardly believe it. In the Boy Scouts I had learned how to plan meals and determined the supplies that I would need for the trip. Curt and I ended up filling the back of his Ford Courier pickup, which we crammed with food, and I mean crammed. We bought what I figured would be enough supplies and food to last three months and in the end it could have lasted about nine months.

February arrived as I prepared to leave Longview for my first stop on this adventure, which would be Astoria, Oregon on the Columbia River. It had been more than a month since I had quit my job and I was anxious to begin this journey. I remember the first trip to Astoria that I had taken several years before. I had a week's vacation and I wanted to sail in the ocean. Sometimes I think fate deals us a rotten hand but you have to make the best of it. The weather before the start of my vacation was sunny and warm with no high winds. This is a rarity for spring in the Pacific Northwest. The week my vacation started so did the rains. After a few days of waiting for the weather to change the impatience of youth got the better of me and I decided to go anyway.

I am not sure why, but some of us learn our lesson from the experiences of others and then there are those like myself who always seem to learn things the hard way. The only good thing I can say about "the hard way" is that once a lesson is learned it is seldom forgotten. By the time I made the twelve-hour passage from Longview to Astoria I was wet and cold. I tied across from the fuel dock at the Port of Astoria and since I was so tired I would wait until morning to leave on my first trip into the ocean. While I was tied to the dock, one of the guys that worked there asked me if I had a bar guide. This is not a guide to the night life but rather a guide on when it is safe to cross the Columbia River Bar. When I told him that I did not have one, he gave me his. I thought that the guide he gave me was fascinating. I really did not know that things like this existed. It had all the compass courses on it from buoy to buoy all the way to the Columbia River Lightship. The Columbia was one of the few rivers marked by a lightship. I was disappointed to find on my later trips offshore that the lightship had been replaced by one of those modern navigational buoys. I will miss seeing the lightship on station.

When I was younger, once I set my mind to do something I did it. Maybe the lessons I learned on this little excursion taught me to weigh the cost of a thing before making a decision. As I got up in the morning I was told that it was a little sloppy outside. Well, the small craft warnings turned to gale warnings while I was offshore. That gave me something to write home about! I still remember the feel as my boat met the ocean swells for the first time. The smell of the salt air added to the sensations as an upper river boy went to sea for the first time.

On the way out over the bar I saw the Coast Guard telling some of the other boats that it would be a good idea if they headed in. They did not stop me. Maybe they thought I knew what I was doing, but were they wrong! The seas continued to build until they were about fifteen feet high with an occasional wave breaking. The forty-knot winds screamed through the rigging. I will not go into detail about the damage my boat incurred on this little outing, but when you fall off large waves time and time again more than your nerves get rattled. After passing Astoria on my return to the Columbia River from the ocean I had to stay at the wheel for twelve hours. All I wanted to do was escape my heaving world. To be rid of the rain, the leaks in the boat, and the other hassles made me press on toward home when a sane person would have stopped. I dreamed of a hot bath, a warm bed, and good food. Once I was safely tied to the dock back home I ended up sleeping for the next fifteen hours and was tired for days afterwards, and that was from just one day at sea. Now years later these thoughts flooded over me as I was once again headed for sea. I wondered what would be in store for me as I put myself into the midst of a force, to me incomprehensible.

2.

OUT TO SEA

MANY OF OUR friends saw us off at Cathlamet and we had not gone very far when Curt asked where all the water was coming from. Somehow the engine drain had become open and since the engine was running, the water was just pouring into the boat. Once the valve was closed and the bilge pump was turned on the boat was once again dry. This was the only mishap to occur on the trip down river to Astoria. At Astoria we called home and told them that we would try to leave in the morning. It was great that Curt was with me because he knew several cool places to see in Astoria. One of the high points of this passage was the steam house where we took a good soak. Not only does it ease all the little aches and pains of the passage, it relaxes you so you sleep really well.

The next morning we released the mooring lines and were starting our adventure. The Columbia River is a very large river and with the tide going out the amount of water leaving the river was hard to believe. Curt suggested that we turn the boat around against the tide and river flow to see if we had the power to hold our own against this force. Sometimes the river can flow at eight knots or more. Well with full power we could just hold our own against the current. That meant that if we passed Ilwaco we would be committed and would be out to sea if we wanted to be or not. As we neared Ilwaco we thought that we saw a sailboat coming in across the bar under full sail. That in itself would not be so strange except we could not make any headway against the ebb tide. We would see the boat through the mist and then a squall line would pass and it would disappear. In a few minutes we would see it again like a phantom ship. As the conditions were deteriorating, we decided to go into Ilwaco. This is one of the ports where local knowledge would have come in real handy. Evening is not the best time to enter port, especially if the channel twists like a snake. I had just bought new charts before we left for this trip so I had every reason to believe that they were correct. They were not; we bumped and then hit hard and leaned over. One lesson I learned the hard way came in handy then. I swung the wheel hard over and as the next wave hit us we lifted and were free. I am sure nearly everyone who has a sailboat has, at one time or another, been aground. I met some people while cruising who must have the record for groundings in a day. Nine times, and I do not think that they have learned their lesson yet.

We plugged in the 200,000 candle power spotlight and with a watchful eye on the fathometer we negotiated the rest of the channel without mishap. As we pulled into Ilwaco I noticed a lighted berth with a bunch of ducks sitting on it. This looked like a good place to tie up. As I brought her in, Curt made ready the lines. He jumped, the ducks scattered, and he slipped on all the duck droppings and almost fell into the water. That would have really topped off his day. Thus, another valuable lesson learned: be careful when you come into a dock occupied by ducks because they leave a part of themselves behind to mark their territory. We moved to another dock! Once we were safely at the dock, we went and treated ourselves to a dinner in the restaurant that overlooked the harbor. We figured that tomorrow was another day and we could try it again in the morning.

Next day Curt and I finally crossed the bar and were in the ocean. When we reached the light buoy, the steering broke and we had to put on the emergency tiller. We talked about it and decided that we should go back to Astoria for repairs. I relied a lot on Curt's judgment. We called home so they would not worry because we had filed a float plan with them. A simple float plan provides all the information that might be needed by authorities if they need to start a search for an overdue vessel. The plan gives a description of the vessel, name of the vessel, and identification numbers. The plan lists the crew aboard by name and address. The plan also states the time and port of departure and estimated arrival time for the next port.

When we were back at the dock, we noticed that a new forty-six-foot sailboat had come in since we were in Astoria the day before. This turned out to be the phantom ship we saw coming in over the bar through the haze. I discovered that the captain of our phantom ship was Fritz Sandoz. His vessel was the *Natural Velocity*. When I first saw Fritz, he was barefoot wearing a Mexican serape and jeans. That in itself is not odd, but when you consider the cold weather and the fact that it was raining, he looked out of place. Fritz had just recently taken possession of his new yacht. He had spent several months in Taiwan overseeing her construction. The *Natural Velocity* was a center cockpit sloop with a king-sized berth in the aft cabin. There was also a head in the aft cabin with a diesel heater that he used as a sauna. Moving forward was a quarter berth for the navigator and the navigation station. The galley was to the port with another diesel heater for the main cabin. Forward of the galley is the U-shaped area with the dining table and an additional seat across from it. Through the next bulkhead was a forward head and another double berth. It was quite a vessel.

The *Natural Velocity* was an impressive vessel, but what

impressed me more than the boat was a chart that Fritz had made while he was in Mexico the year before. Fritz had been cruising on his previous boat, which was the same size as mine. Fritz's visa had expired and he had to leave the country. Since he did not want to sail back to the States he decided to sail to Hawaii. The only problem was that his charts of Hawaii were back in Winchester Bay, Oregon. What did Fritz do you ask? He turned a chart over and, with the help of a coast pilot, made his own chart by creating the grid of latitudes and longitudes from Mexico to Hawaii. Every day on his passage you would see the different notes that he would make on the chart. An example of one entry is, "hot chess game, forgot to take noon sight." I was fascinated to see what he had done. Since we were both going the same direction, we decided that we would try to keep in radio contact.

The wind was not cooperating and after several days we could not take being just fifty miles from home, so we raised sail and went home. It was a good sail back home, but I was sad in the fact that I was going home and would have to meet all the people again that saw me off. It was a disappointing time for me more than Curt. **Curt was in love**.

I know now why so many sailors hate to have to reenter a port they have left on a voyage. All of your thoughts and energies are directed toward that "next port." For me it was especially so. I had quit my job and tried to leave on a certain date. I changed the date several times and when it looked like I would get to finally leave the weather did not cooperate. I wondered if I would ever get to leave on the trip!

The week while waiting out the weather I kept to myself. I did not call my friends or even see them. I became a hermit. I might have felt ashamed, but I do not really know the words that describe how I felt. Discouraged, disappointed, and maybe even a little like a failure. I will leave it by saying that I did not feel good! The week that I was back home I paid a lot of attention to the weather reports and what the pattern seemed to be doing. Weather in the Pacific Northwest during the winter can be unpredictable.

As Curt and I sailed back home, we heard that the wind had swung around to the Northwest. That was the wind that several of us at Astoria were waiting for. We were just sure that Fritz would be on his way to Winchester Bay. One of my first lessons about weather forecasting was learned during my time in Astoria. For those of you who do not know, you can not always believe what NOAA weather is saying. So there I was back in Longview waiting for the wind to cooperate.

3.
THE START OF A DREAM

I CONSIDER MYSELF lucky that I grew up where I did. Since my family never left the area, I had time to enjoy everything that this rural community had to offer. The city is spreading out our way, but twenty-five years ago is the way I will always remember it. My two older brothers, my younger sister, and I all had a terrific amount of freedom when we were growing up. There were two main areas that we played at. First was Mt. Solo, with its caves, animals, and everything else that the woods had to offer. I will never forget the times we would spend the afternoons climbing the mountains. Mt. Solo would not even be considered a mountain. It is not much higher than the surrounding lowlands but when you are eight years old the view from the top is something I will always remember. I would look down and try to pick out the different houses and cars, all of which looked like toys or something from *Gulliver's Travels*.

The other main place where we played while growing up were the sloughs that are reached by walking through the nut and apple orchards. The sloughs were built for flood control and connected the Cowlitz River to the Columbia River. They were fresh flowing during my youth but today are nearly all covered over. We spent many days boating, fishing, and swimming in them.

Anything that would float was put into service just so we could be out on the water. I can still remember some of the dreams that I dreamed as a child on those waters. We made rafts without number and if they sank or drifted away, we would just build another. I will never forget the time I got into trouble for using a concrete mixing trough that my dad had. My dad worked construction so this would be considered one of his tools, a big no-no. The trough was about five feet long, three feet wide, and eight inches high on the sides. You know how kids are always thinking. Well, I thought that this would make a terrific boat. When my dad found out about it, as fathers always do, he was not happy. That mixing trough never took another trip down the sloughs. After this incident dad decided he would help us build a real boat, which ended up being an eight foot pram that my dad had the jigs for. With my dad's help this became THE boat and dad even got us a three-horse-power Johnson outboard motor for it.

In the center of Longview is a manmade lake called Lake Sacajawea. When I was eleven my parents opened a boat rental at the lake. We rented canoes, rowboats and paddle wheel scooters, and our chase boat was that famous eight-foot pram with its Johnson outboard. I have stored many fond memories of the warm summer days spent on the lake. I think that when our lives are over, all we have left are the memories that we have stored, whether they be good ones or bad. The good thing about time is that it softens the bad memories, and if we are lucky we can relive the warm sunny days and be transported to our yesterday and a simpler time.

As I was reliving the memories of my youth NOAA was promising Northwest winds, so on March 31st we are headed back to Astoria. We entered port and were surprised to find the *Natural Velocity* still at Astoria. Fritz told us that one of his crew members had abandoned ship when he came into port and that the other crewmember had been with his newfound friend since the *Natural Velocity* had entered port. The week that we were back home, Fritz had sailed to Longview too, visiting friends. So there we all were, waiting for the Northwest winds together. When I go into port the first thing I do is make sure the boat is shipshape. I even made a coconut cream pie, which was a first. I was never really big on cooking but I decided that if I did not want to starve, I would have to learn how to cook. There are not any McDonalds around the corner when you are at sea. Curt and I were invited to have dinner aboard Fritz's boat that night, Mexican food, who would have guessed? They made enough food for an army. With the appetite that the sea gave us, we became an army. The four of us left nary a scrap.

After dinner Curt and I went to see a movie, *Earthbound,* which Curt thought was terrible. The next stop was a steam bath, which we both enjoyed. Then it was back to the boat to see what tomorrow would hold for us. We woke shortly after eight in the morning and when Fritz and Les came over at eight-thirty I gave them the last two pieces of pie. We topped off our water tanks and motored over to the fuel docks to meet Fritz and Les. With the promise of Northwest winds, I called home to say that we were leaving again. I hoped.

4.

ON OUR WAY

FRITZ AND I planned to keep in radio contact, not only for safety, but so I could learn from his experience. By 0900 we were motoring at five knots for the open sea, and raised sail. The dance that the boat does as she meets the sea is different from that on any other body of water. Because the *Natural Velocity* is a larger vessel, we soon fell in behind her. It was something to watch her rise to meet the waves and then disappear behind the next one as we ourselves rose to climb each peak and then slide down to the valley. I still can not believe how five minutes of time can change the face of the Columbia River Bar. We were finally on our way and, Lord willing, the next stop will be Newport, Oregon.

Curt took the watch from noon until 4 p.m. My watch will last from 4 p.m. till 10 p.m. I was starting to get a complex. Whenever Curt was on watch, we seemed to have more wind and make better time than when I was on watch. When we were not on watch, most of the time we would try to sleep. When I got out of bed to relieve Curt at two in the morning I was in a different world. I had never seen so many stars nor had they ever been more brilliant than they were this night. I thought that I could reach out and touch them. People who have never been at sea before cannot imagine how bright the stars are. On land you have smog and light pollution that cut down the stars' visibility a tremendous amount. At sea away from the shore you can see stars touching the water all around you. I will never forget this sight.

Curt was really terrific. We both ate a fair amount of junk food at sea. About three in the morning a squall came through and soaked me. The temperature was about forty degrees. You cannot sail without wind, but this was one time that I was wishing that we were becalmed. The wind drove right through me—even with my foul weather gear on, and this is definitely what I would call foul weather. I had to keep telling myself that this is fun. It is funny, but nothing is ever like it is in the movies. With any luck, we would reach Newport in the morning. For some reason during the night the depth sounder decided to go on strike. I was glad that my brother Craig had talked me into putting a battery isolator switch on board because two of my three batteries went dead during the night. I thought it was fatigue at first, Murphy's law, I suppose, but it did not take the engine long to charge the batteries back to one hundred percent.

Newport was to be just the first of many unfamiliar ports at which I would call. The passage south from Astoria was just slow enough that we caught the tide when it was ebbing. This was the first and last time I would try to enter a port when the tide was going out. Under full sail and power, I thought that I saw ants on the jetty making better headway than we were. Just inside the bridge that spans the harbor entrance was a new marina. We pulled into a slip, and a young man was waiting at the dock to meet us. He said that he had been watching us since the point. We asked him how far it was to town and he suggested that the other marina was much closer to town. We started the engine and invited him to motor over with us to the other marina. With our new-found guide aboard, we chugged through the hundreds of boats and, lo and behold, almost at the end of the dock was the *Natural Velocity*. There was an empty slip just a few boats down from her so we tied up and exchanged sailing strategies. You see, we had not heard from them since we lost sight of them after leaving Astoria. They had sailed even farther offshore to try to catch the promised Northwest winds on the outer fringes of a gale. I was happy to have this challenging passage behind me. When I have my boat safely tied to the dock I feel the pride of a job well done. You can read the Coast Pilot, look at the different cruising books, study the charts, etc., but they just do not show how a port will look in real life.

After dinner aboard *Maranatha*, Curt and Les went to town to check out the local watering hole. It was getting dark and I went to make a call. I called home and told them that all was well. It had started raining again and as I walked down the dock, I saw *Mary* smiling, golden light coming from her ports. I wish I could describe the warm feeling that it gave me. I opened the hatch to the aft cabin and was in my own world. Warm, dry and being sung to sleep by the sounds of water lapping the sides of her hull. A note of interest is that Newport is a free port. This was the only port I have called at that did not charge for overnight moorage.

5.
THE CHALLENGES AT SEA

IT WAS EIGHT in the morning and we were making ready to get under way and leave Newport. I was really not very excited to be going to sea again so soon, having not really rested from the passage down from Astoria. Somewhere in the back of my mind there was the thought that there is safety in numbers. I was sure that if the *Natural Velocity* was not leaving port today, I would not be either. At best, there was a false sense of security because the radio on the *Natural Velocity* has been on the blink and the difference in size and speed would make it impossible for me to keep up with her.

It has been said that if you fall off a horse you should get right back on or you will lose your nerve. Maybe that is what we were doing. In one respect, it was a good thing that we were leaving. I think that if you lose your courage on a voyage, where you are when that takes place is likely to be the place your voyage will end. I am sure that you have heard of someone sailing to a particular destination and when they arrive they end up selling their boat there. That is enough said about that.

We cleared the outer buoy at nine in the morning and our destination was to be Winchester Bay. As we raised sail, it seemed that things started to fall apart. This was one of those days that I was thinking that I should have stayed in bed. The wind was gusting pretty well and we jibbed. That is something you are not supposed to do. It is when the sails come across the boat and reset on the opposite tack. The boomed working jib came across and hit the bow pulpit. What was left of the boom could now be used for fender boards, kindling or whatever I decided to do with the piece of wood shattered in numerous pieces. You could say that this was the straw that broke the camel's back. I completely lost control of myself and started to swear a blue streak. I told God that if he was not going to help me, at least he did not have to work against me. All the while that I was having my tantrum, Curt just stood by and smiled. He did not say a word. I have never met anyone with more patience than Curt. Keep in mind that we had just cleared the outer buoy. My day was not starting well at all. Then I felt guilty, more about losing control than about the swearing. After we cleared away the broken boom, we were on our way again. We were moving at a real good clip, six knots and sometimes up to seven knots. That is pretty good for a boat with a twenty-two-foot waterline.

Other that the jib boom breaking, we did not have any other problems on the sail to Winchester Bay. I even tried to get the boat to self-steer a little on the way south, without much success I might add. At 11 p.m. we were laying off Winchester Bay. I called the Coast Guard to find out about the bar conditions and they offered to guide us across because of the difficulty of the entrance. I asked them if they had heard anything from the *Natural Velocity* and they said that they were cut off in the middle of transmission. Their last reported position was about one mile west from where we were. We saw a light in that direction and asked them if they wanted us to check it out? As we neared the light we saw the *Natural Velocity* and pulled next to Fritz. He asked us to relay the message to the Coast Guard that he was going to heave to until morning and then come in. This I did and we decided to heave to also and wait till morning. This was my first experience in heaving to, and on the other occasions I have done it, it has gone much the same. There must be some trick to doing it that I have not learned yet. The motion is not much different from that of riding a roller coaster or mechanical bull. The main difference is that everything in the boat seems to change from one side to the other side while you are bouncing around. When you are moving through the water the forces on your boat are balanced out by your sails. If you are just sitting there, your sail acts as a pendulum and you are the part that swings.

By two-thirty in the morning I could not stand it any more and set a course for Coos Bay. By 5 a.m. I was so tired I could not keep a compass course. It would have been funny if I had not been in the mood I was in. I would watch the compass spin around for a while before it would dawn on me that I was off course. I had to have Curt relieve me so I could get some sleep. If you have ever been too tired to sleep, you know how I felt. I just lay there on Curt's bunk and started to get chilled. This can be a major problem at sea. You get run down and then hypothermia can set in. I am sure that many accidents at sea can be attributed to these causes.

During this time something that Curt said began weighing on my mind. He said "the risks involved in sailing outweighed the benefits" as far as he was concerned. I knew that this meant that he would leave before too long. I just hoped that he would stay until we reached San Francisco.

I have heard it said that we dream every night. I will not try to deny that. I will just clarify that for me by saying that the only dreams that I remember are what you might call visions. The dreams that I remember seem to come true. In the back of my mind I always knew that I would take this trip alone. I at least am grateful for all the things that Curt taught me. Sometime in the middle of the night I got up to relieve Curt at the wheel. As I grabbed the wheel house to steady myself, I broke the wire that powers the night lighting for the compass. I did not say a word; I just turned around and went back to bed. I do not know what I would have done if Curt had not been there to relieve me.

When the sun started to come up I relieved Curt and took a watch. By six thirty in the morning we were eight miles southwest of where we should have been. This was due, in part I am sure, to our heaving to but most likely to my great steering as we went in circles during the night. At seven thirty in the morning we were at the outer buoy and by chance we hit the tide right. I was really glad to be tied safely to the dock by eight in the morning. After calling home to let them know we were safe and sound I could finally get some sleep.

6.

NEEDED REPAIRS

COOS BAY, OR Charleston to be more specific, was an eventful port for me in many ways. Ever since we left the Columbia River we had been taking on quite a lot of water. We were having to pump the boat every four hours and more often if there were any seas at all. Not far from Astoria we hit something real hard that was in the water. It must have been a sinker, that is, a submerged log. The Mt. St. Helens eruption ended up sending a lot of junk down the river. Well after hitting whatever it was we hit, we started taking on water. I made the determination that I could not live with the leak any more. I was hoping, as we all do sometimes, that the problem would fix itself. You know, they hardly ever do.

I do not think that I could have found a better port on the entire Oregon coast for repairs although I did not know it at the time. There are two marine ways in the Coos Bay area. The one that I chose was just on the other side of the bridge that leads to Coos Bay. Since the bridge is manned, a few toots on the horn and you are at the ways ready to be hauled out. This particular ways could handle boats up to sixty-five feet and unlike many marine yards they would let you do your own work and did not put pressure on you whatever you chose to do. If you should need any parts or materials they could be found within easy walking distance. The cost for my boat was twenty-five dollars a day and that included haul-out and re-launching.

I do not care how much you love your boat, there are times that you need to get away from the problems that are associated with it. For some reason, a lot of people think that all you do if you are cruising is sail. They could not be more wrong. I was finding out that a major part of cruising was the maintenance that you have to do. I am sure there are those who do not do the little jobs that have to be done when they need to be done. I have sailed on more than one vessel where the skipper had let things slide and all that I will say is that I would not want to be in a situation where my life depended on the equipment that was not working. I have found that it is much easier if you do the little jobs as they come up. I do have to admit that if we had not left in the stormy season there would not have been nearly as much upkeep as I was having to do. While I was on the ways, I felt that for my own sanity I had to have a change of pace and get away from the pain of all the repairs I had to do.

It seems as if everyone in the world is becoming colder and more detached from his fellow man. You do not see people going out of their way to help each other. Not only in the boating community, but it seems everywhere in the world, the sense of community is disappearing. I think that is why I was so overwhelmed by the many kindnesses that were shown to me in this most friendly port. Just one example of what I mean is the night I needed to get away. I felt like going to see the town, take in a movie, and eat someone's cooking other than my own.

The main town of Coos Bay is about ten miles from where the marine ways are. I had mentioned to the owner of the yard that I would like to go to town that night and asked him where a good place was to eat. He not only suggested several places, he volunteered to give me a ride to town. He became my tour guide and pointed out several different places to eat, and drove me to different movie houses so I could check out which movie I would like to see. He even offered to take me to the neighboring town if I did not find anything that looked interesting to me. As I was getting out of his car having made my choice, I asked him where he lived? He said that he lived right above the ways. That meant that he had gone more than twenty miles out of his way just to make me feel welcome in his town. His kindness reminded me of the bible story about going that extra mile.

Unlike many ports along the Pacific Coast, all of the cruisers' needs were located within easy walking distance, including the first thing everyone looks for after clearing into a port...the showers. I have never seen any quite like the ones here. The building was divided into two sides is how I would describe it. On one side were the private restrooms. They had big mirrors and were well lit. On the other side were the private showers. For a mere quarter you could let the hot water ease the aches of a rough passage and drive the chill from your bones.

The damage I discovered on the ways was far worse than what I had expected to find. The shaft log was loose as well as the strut. Those are the parts that hold the shaft from the engine to the prop that propels the vessel. There was some separation where we had hit whatever it was in the water that night. I discovered that the quadrant, which connects to the rudder that steers the boat, had a crack in it when I pulled out the shaft to have it checked for true. I found that the prop was just hanging by a thread. That meant that the end of the shaft had to be cut off and then drilled and tapped for a bolt to hold the prop on. That turned out to be a mighty expensive log I hit and I did not even get any firewood out of the deal.

Our first night in port Curt and I went to a real nice restaurant for dinner. I did not feel much like cooking that night. The restaurant was built out overlooking the water. While we were waiting for our dinner to be served, we noticed that there were several people out on the mud flats. It was low tide and we discovered that they were digging clams. Since Curt had been a commercial fisherman, I just knew that he would have no problem limiting out the next day. I felt that something had been bothering Curt from the time he had mentioned the risks we faced being at sea this time of year. When he was commercial fishing he was at least compensated with money for the risks he took. The only rewards so far on this adventure were cold watches during the middle of the night and living in a damp space smaller than convicts have in solitary confinement. It would be a different world when we got to the warm weather, but sometimes all we can see is what is immediately in front of us. That meant at least four hundred more miles until we would see any warm weather.

During our dinner Curt came out and said what I had been afraid he was going to say. The next port was to be his last. For me it really put a damper on the evening's festivities. You know I did not blame him at all for his decision. I could think of a lot more fun things to do on a vacation than spend it in rough seas. And remember, Curt had someone back home whom he not only loved but who loved him in return. I knew that if I had what he had I would have never left. There is no better feeling than that of being in love.

The next day, being Sunday, I decided to go to church as is my custom when I am in port. It does not matter to me by what name the church is called, for we all worship the same God. I believe that if you have an open mind you will receive something from every service you attend and this was no exception. The insight that the pastor gave on The Last Supper really impressed me. I was glad I went.

As I was making lunch on the boat, Joe and Connie Bush dropped by to see me. I had met them in church that morning. I must have seemed rude to them. I did not even ask them aboard. I would not have blamed them if they never came back. I felt ashamed afterwards of how cold I had been to them. I am not like that. I was starting to be in a bad mood and it took me a while to figure out why. It was loneliness and something more. I felt a loss because Curt was going to leave. Try and visualize what it is like. You leave your job, all your friends and family, and in short everything that gives stability to your life. Every time you leave a port you leave behind any new friends that you have made and you are going to a place that you have never been before and where you do not know anyone. I would learn later that stability in my life would come from within, but at this point in my life I felt lost.

There are times when I think I am not the sharpest tool in the shed. During the time I have been on the voyage water has gotten into the knot meter. Like an odometer on a car it tells how fast you are going and the distance you have traveled. I figured that the perfect thing to get the moisture out of the knot meter would be a heat lamp I had on board. Instead of drying out the knot meter what I succeeded in doing was melting the numbers in the dial. In addition to that when I turned the heat lamp off the moisture inside of the knot meter was worse than when I started. Now it looked like a fog bank had taken up residence inside. So much for that great idea.

All day our mouths had been watering at the thought of clam chowder and since the tide was out now, Curt was eager to get to those little hummers, the clams. I saw him walk off with bucket and shovel in hand. I could hardly wait for his return. In about half an hour I spotted Curt coming back with a huge grin on his face. I was thinking that he would have a bucket full since he knew the ropes, so to speak. When I looked in the bucket I was informed that the clams did not have anything to worry about from us. No clams. I do not know anyone who has worse luck at anything having to do with fishing than me. Maybe my luck has rubbed of on Curt or is contagious. I did not know if Curt would remember this clamming expedition, but the look on Curt's face when he said, "No clams," is something that I never will forget. He was, as they say, skunked!

After the clamming incident, Curt changed his clothes and left. I ate alone tonight and was amazing myself with the fact that I was really learning to cook. Curt came back aboard at eleven-thirty at night and asked if I would wake him at five in the morning. He was going home in the morning. On land everything is shades of gray. At sea life is black and white. You take the time to examine your life and your values to decide what is important to you. Curt said that he discovered what was important to him. He had something to go back home to, Lucy and her kids. I did not blame him at all. I wished I had what he had.

My mind was flooded with all the fears of having to make it alone. There is no way I can let you know how I felt right then. The only word I can think of that describes how I felt is empty at the thought of Curt leaving.

7.

ALONE

AT COOS BAY, as it would be at every other port where I spent any length of time, I found that there would be certain people with whom I am predestined to become friends. It was almost as if God had prepared them for me to ease my loneliness and make me feel at home. There are two families whom I am close to at Coos Bay: Ken and Shirley Gardner, who own a charter boat service, and Joe and Connie Bush. I can hardly believe all the things Joe and I had in common. We were both pastors at one time, and for different reasons had each given up our pastorate. When Joe was young he had gone with his father on a cruise to Mexico. The experience of that voyage gave him a real understanding of the problems and emotions of cruising and being separated from friends and family. Joe's dad wrote a book about their adventures which I got to read. I got a kick out of seeing the pictures of Joe when he was a boy. The memories he had of that cruise made him hope to one day be back working with simple peasants along the Mexican coast.

I will never forget the Bushes' kindness to me. Many times I was invited over to their house for dinner and was captivated by the beauty of his watercolors. When I returned home I read an article in one of the papers featuring Joe down at the docks painting. I was having a good deal of problems with the wind vane on *Mary* and Joe and I set out to remedy those problems. I have to admit now that it was a hopeless case. I think that the best thing about the wind vane was when it went overboard while I was cruising the Delta. Joe and I went to different stores and bought the necessary things we thought might remedy the wind vane's inherent problems. For all the materials we bought Joe would not let me pay a dime. My money was not any good as long as I was with him. I am still amazed by his giving nature and selflessness. Here he was spending money for something that he would never be benefited by. What it showed me was his love.

The ten days that I had been in Coos Bay I spent many hours wondering if it would be my last port. I was having a hard time even with the help of Curt and I really did not think that I would be able to handle the long times that I would have to be at the wheel since there would be no one to relieve me. I started a practice that I would follow the remainder of my cruising days. Before I would leave port I would write down on paper the different compass courses I should steer and the distances between different landmarks or ports. In general I would have all the information done ahead of time in case I was a slave to the wheel. In addition to that I had read everything that the different books I had would have to say about the upcoming ports. The Oregon and Washington coasts are not very hospitable. You might have to go hundreds of miles to reach a safe port. Those who do not cruise up north can not visualize what an ebb tide does to the different river bars. There are times when the Columbia River is even closed to ship traffic. I also checked with the Coast Guard to get bar guides, and whatever information I could in hopes that it would decrease the danger involved in sailing the coast this time of year.

While at Coos Bay I met Al Schaeffer. I ran over to his house one day to look at the forty-seven-foot sailboat he was building.

When I saw it I was surprised to discover that it was just a shell. Hearing him talk about how he was going to finish her out brought back a flood of memories from when I built *Mary*.

I think that the dream of having a boat and sailing away started to take form in my mind when I was having trouble in my marriage. I do not know if just the thought of escaping to a simpler life is what interested me most or not. But I am sure that it was a big part of it. I am sure that all of us at one time or another wish we could just run away from the pressures of problems we face every day. If we cannot escape them, it would just be a relief to be free from the pressures for time to rest.

At the time I started building my boat. I was working night crew at a major grocery chain. The long hours that I put into the boat made it so I did not have to be confronted by my wife and argue. Looking back on this time I think I made a bad choice because being away as much as I was may have contributed to the problems we were having at the time and ultimately led her to find comfort from someone else. I have never been successful in this area of my life—personal relationships with the opposite sex. I may never be!

While building the boat I was also pastoring the Oak Point Community Church. I have to say that this was the most fulfilling time in my life. I felt that I could give of myself to others and make a difference in their lives. My spirit suffered two great losses at this time. My high school sweetheart and wife left me and because of that I had to resign my pastorate at Oak Point. The organization that licensed me to pastor stated that I could no longer be the pastor of the church. They said that if I could not rule my own house I should not try to rule God's house. I am glad that I never felt like God had deserted me. In spite of all that has happened, God still loves me!

Before I decided on the twenty-six-foot Morning Star design I was interested in others as well. Because I had not been on any large sailboats I was not real sure how much boat I needed. I made the right decision with the boat plans I ended up choosing, and I am pleased with *Mary*.

Over the next two and one-half years I would put all of my energies into building *Mary*. I would end up sleeping about four hours a day. I think that to a great extent, I was trying to fill the emptiness that was in my life. That and the fact that I do not do anything halfway. I am generally an all-or-nothing type of person. I have not quite decided whether that is a good or bad thing. I have just accepted it as part of who I am.

I do not know if I will ever build another boat. When I think back on all that is involved in the process it is almost hard to imagine that I really did it. Several years ago there were companies that sold boat hulls that the owner could finish out. What most people do not realize is that the hull of a boat only represents about ten percent of the completed project. There are literally hundreds of details that need to be figured out to finish building a boat. Just think, like a house you have plumbing, wiring, cooking facilities, sleeping quarters, engine installation, and a host of details that all need to be worked out and finished. I am sure that we have all seen the skeletons of someone's dream that has died sitting abandoned in someone's backyard or barn. I am grateful that I was able to finish what I started. I could talk about the mistakes I had made while building *Mary*. Things that I had to fix and the difficulty in figuring out how to build one of the components. Many times I changed my mind on how I wanted a particular section to be when finished. I do not think that anyone can fully understand what it takes to build a boat unless he or she has gone through this experience.

After I looked at Al's boat and checked with the Coast Guard I was as ready as I thought I could be. I put my faith in a power far greater than mine. I believe that you do all that you can do, and the rest has to be a step of faith. The day before I left port, Joe and I tried out the modified wind vane without much success. With some shock cord and surgical tubing of different links we were able to come up with a combination that would prove to work with at least a moderate amount of success.

I had a dream before I left on the trip of me being in a terrible storm with mountainous seas. The dream seemed so real and I vividly remember the fear that I felt. I did not see death, but then I woke up terrified and never finished the dream. These thoughts were in the back of my mind as I let the lines go that held me to a secure world where I could step off if I was tired. The next port would be Brookings with any luck at all. It would mean an eighty-six mile run and about eighteen hours at the wheel.

8.

FIRST SOLO PASSAGE

BY APRIL FOURTEENTH I was ready to leave port, or should I say that the boat was ready for sea? I was not too sure if I was ready or not. In the back of my mind I was haunted by my dream. In the dream I was in mountainous seas with the wind screaming through the rigging. I remember the fear I felt as the seas were crashing down on me. The thought of being in conditions like that unsettled me.

The sun was still asleep as I got ready to leave port. When I cast off the lines it was six-thirty in the morning. Both the sun and I were ready for another day. For me the early morning has a special peace all its own. As I looked out over the water there was a layer of fog just above the water that it made it seem like I was sailing in the clouds instead of on the water.

I had planned to keep in touch with Ken and Shirley Gardner, aboard their charter boat the *Betty K*. Even though I tried every half hour, I was never able to reach them by VHF radio.

As the morning melted into afternoon, my body became like a sponge soaking up the warmth that the sun put out. Up till then, the weather had been cold offshore. I played with the self-steering gear and by some miracle it was holding course and steering. As the sun warmed me I dozed off, lying on a cockpit cushion with cold Kool-Aid to drink. I really appreciated having refrigeration aboard. Every now and then I would check the horizon to see if I was still on course. Each time I checked I was amazed to find that she still was. I was sailing at five and one-half knots and for six hours I was freed from the drudgery of being tied to the wheel. I could cat-nap, cook, read or do anything else I wanted to. To many this is how they envision sailing to be. You can not always believe everything that Hollywood portrays in the movies as the truth. This sail will always be special to me, because it is how I thought that sailing was supposed to be and it was my first real passage offshore alone. I could not have been more pleased with the performance of *Mary* that day.

I arrived at Brookings seventeen hours after clearing Coos Bay. When I had her safely tied to the docks I called home and then went to sleep. The next morning I scouted out the town and ate breakfast at one of the local diners. To me, every port has a common feel about it. The same activities taking place, which makes you feel like you have been there before. Boats are still being worked on, fishermen are busy at the tasks all fishermen do, and the only thing that seems to change is the setting where these activities are taking place.

9.

CALIFORNIA

I AM ALWAYS amazed at how the mood to sea can change so fast. I left Brookings at seven in the morning for Crescent City. The winds were from the south again, which would mean a wet trip as anyone who has beat windward in the choppy seas can tell you. The previous day was so nice that I was shocked at the weather that day. The wind was blowing thirty knots and was causing quite a chop to build up. The predominant wind and wave pattern along this part of the Pacific coast is supposed to be from the northwest so when the wind changes direction it makes the sea a mess. The ten to fourteen-foot waves are bad enough by themselves, but it is not the size of the waves that really matter—it is how close the waves are to one another. The difference between a fifteen-second interval and a five-second interval is night and day. The wind can also be so strong that it blows the tops of the waves off. Today I had both. High waves at close intervals and waves being blown off into my face. More than once water would come over the bow and give me a shower in the cockpit, which is about eighteen feet from the bow.

I learned my first lesson about reefs today. When I picture a reef, I think about the kind I have seen in Hawaii. Well, not all reefs are like that. The reefs off the Oregon and northern California coast are just rocks sticking up out of the water. Sometimes these reefs extend out well over ten miles from shore. I took pictures of an abandoned lighthouse on the end of one of these reefs, which was twelve miles from the mainland. I am sure now that I would have had a smoother passage if I had been further from the reefs offshore. When the ocean floor rises as it approaches landfall the shallow water around the reef makes the sea dance.

I had most of my canned goods stored under the cockpit. Being in a hurry getting ready to leave on the trip I did not shellac the cans to help prevent rusting. I can use that as an excuse, but the main reason was that I am lazy. On the deck were cowl vents for the bilge blower. Gasoline-powered boats need these vents to remove any fumes from the bilge of the boat to prevent an explosion. Because I had a diesel engine these vents were not necessary but I did not take the time to remove them. I knew that I must have taken fifty gallons of seawater down these vents during this passage and that I would end up with a lot of rusty cans. I guess this keeps in line with the fact that I learn my lessons the hard way. The passage from Brookings to Crescent City only took six hours at sea and I was ready to enter my first California port.

I was going to celebrate by drinking a bottle of champagne that Mike and Joan Wey gave me when I left on the trip, but I thought it would be better if I saved it for the time when we could share it together. They were planning to visit me at San Francisco. I called home and shared my excitement at making Crescent City with my family and friends and then headed for a steak dinner at a restaurant that overlooked the harbor.

There are two things I saw at Crescent City that made an impression on me. The first was the carvings of mermaids and dolphins near the harbor office, and the other was a plaque that was dedicated to the fisherman who had lost their lives at sea from this port. This reminded me of the awesome power of the sea and the danger involved in what I was doing. Although I did not realize it at the time, I would later understand what Curt meant when he said that "the risk was too great."

10.

CRAB POTS

I DO NOT consider myself a superstitious person, but I decided to leave in the morning rather than wait and rest up the day in port. You see the next day would be Good Friday. If you remember the story of the Flying Dutchman, you will know what I am talking about. I figured why tempt fate.

By the time I fueled up and was ready to leave port it was eleven o'clock in the morning. At least I got to sleep in. I left with a light northwest breeze, which died in about an hour, so it looked as if this would be a motoring affair. *Mary* absolutely refused to self-steer that day; I guess she didn't want to spoil me. Depending on the time of year and where you are, you are liable to see hundreds of crab buoys marking where the crab pots have been set by the fishermen. They remind me of the story of Hansel and Gretel, or of the Wizard of Oz, and following the yellow brick road. How they work is that there are two buoys with a line between them. The fishing boats will come alongside and grab the line between the buoys and haul the crab pot up with their boom. Sometimes you can see both of the buoys and sometimes the current is so strong that you can only see one of them, or maybe none of them. All of the buoys start out the season painted bright colors, which identify whose crab pots they belong to. As the season drags on these buoys become covered with slime and harder to see. I wondered what would happen if someone was to run over one of these buoys. Well, I would not have to wonder any longer. Off of Trinidad Head in the dark, I ran over one. It naturally got fouled in the prop, and I was held there as if I had dropped anchor. A crab pot weighs about one hundred pounds. I radioed the Coast Guard at Humboldt Bay, which is Eureka, and told them the good news. Since the seas were not very large I decided to try to get the crab pot line free from the prop and rudder. I took a boat hook and after making sure that my lifeline was secure I leaned over the boat and grabbed the line with the boat hook. The boat was bobbing like a cork on the waves and for a minute I thought that I would drown. As each wave lifted and dropped the boat I would get dunked underwater and my only watch for navigation would get a swimming lesson. I was certain that the next wave would send me under water. I was afraid to let go of the boat hook which I used to snag the crab pot line with because I did not want to end up losing it. With a strength I did not know I had, I finally got the crab pot line secured to a cleat. I thought that I could use a sheet winch to raise the crab pot and claim any crabs I might find as a prize for all the hassles it cost me. I had been struggling with the crab pot for three hours and I still did not have it aboard. I felt like I was at the limit of my strength. Out came the knife and I cut the line. At least I had one of the buoys on board as a souvenir of my ordeal. Everything ached and I could not remember when I had felt so tired. In my own words, I felt like death warmed over.

The wind was so light I could only make about three knots, but at least the wind was from the right direction. I was so tired that I became disoriented. I could not find the range markers for Eureka. After talking to the Coast Guard, I discovered that I was two miles from the sea buoy. Because of my delay with the crab pot, the tide had turned and there was no way I could come in against an ebb tide. The Coast Guard vessel number 44396 offered to take me in tow. They gave me a drogue to deploy as we crossed the bar. The drogue is a tire with a chain and a line on it that you drag behind your boat to keep you from overtaking the tow vessel. Well, as we neared the bar I tossed the drogue over the side. This was quite a feat in itself because I was being towed at nine knots, which is almost twice as fast as my hull speed. The problem with my boat and maybe all boats is that as your hull speed increases so does the weather helm. I felt like I needed two men and a boy to keep *Mary* under control. You can not believe how fast nine knots is. Well I got the drogue away, but before I could secure the line on the cleat it got away from me. The Coast Guard was not too thrilled when I tell them what happened to their drogue. I figured it must have cost them about one hundred dollars for the drogue. Within an hour, I was safely tied to a dock again. The Coast Guard then boarded me and did a safety inspection. Guess what, I passed! Keep in mind that it is now three thirty in the morning. I think the term, "I crashed," is real accurate. As I went to sleep, I ,was thinking that the worst was yet to come. The passage from Eureka to San Francisco. In the morning I put my air tanks on and cleared the fouled prop. There wrapped around the prop beside the crab line was another buoy. Now I had two green and blue buoys to remind me of my experience off Trinidad Head.

11.

THE BROTHERHOOD OF CRUISERS

STRANGE AS IT may sound, my real introduction into the cruising community came at Eureka. Up until then, all it seemed I had been doing was sailing. Someone told me that for every day at sea, they spend twenty days in port. Well, we all know that had not been the case with me. Up until then, it seemed all I did in port was sleep or do repairs. That is not what I would call having a wild time in port.

Before I left on the trip I bought a cruising guide by Carolyn and Jack West. Since the printing was in 1974, I assumed it would be fairly accurate. In their book, they mentioned the new marina at Eureka that was almost complete. In the book there were photographs of the marina. When I arrived at the new marina, it looked like the photograph in the book. I mean, exactly like it. In the seven years since the photo was taken not much had changed. The marina still was not finished. There was no power to the docks or water. The harbor master was very kind to me and showed me around the facilities. They let me do my laundry there and take a nice long shower, and since the pay boxes were not installed yet, it did not cost me anything. During my stay at Eureka I did get to see the beautiful marina open, although it still was not finished.

I planned to cram a lot into my first day in port. Right across from the new marina were several sailboats rafted together. One of the people on them called me over. His name was Rick Dahlgren of the *La Paloma*. It is kind of funny, but you seem to keep meeting some of the same people time and again in different ports along the way. Many cruisers sailing south or other directions, for that matter, keep running into each other in the various harbors along the way. Just like an exodus everyone seems to be traveling in the same direction. This will be the case with the *La Paloma* and myself. The neat thing about that is when you pull into a strange port and see a familiar face, you feel right at home.

My first day in port I got to see what they call a kinetic sculpture race. It is hard to believe how strange some of the contraptions that were racing looked. Each craft had to have at least two people in it, and they had to travel on the sand, over water, and on city streets. The vehicles were man- or woman-powered, and it appeared that they all had ample room set aside for refreshments aboard their craft. The race was held over a three-day period, and even if they did not win on a particular day, they were not feeling any pain, as the saying goes.

The costumes they wore were as colorful as the machines that they rode. There were people dressed as Norsemen, cavemen, and everything in between all the way to the participants who were wearing formal gowns and tuxedos. Each day's activities ended with a party.

The officials of the race were dressed as Keystone cops. If the racers were caught cheating or disobeying the law, they would be fined, with time being added to that particular leg of the race. My first full day in port was a memorable one!

I remember seeing a movie many years ago about Robin Graham and his voyage aboard the *Dove*. In one scene in the movie, he said that he noticed a difference in the feel of the boat while he was asleep. He woke up to discover that he was off course. I wondered how that could be with all the motion there is on a small boat. How can anyone sense a difference in the feel while they are asleep? The marina where I was staying was so full that I was rafted next to commercial fishing boat. During the night I woke up because something felt wrong. I came out of the hatch and found that the fishermen were moving my boat so that they could go out to get crab pots. There was no noise. They just undid the mooring lines and pulled me along to the next boat in line. By now, I was in tune with my boat and just like Robin in the movie, I could feel the difference even asleep.

I have always heard a reported animosity between commercial fishermen and the so-called yachters. I found that the fisherman always went out of their way to teach me from their experience. They would tell me good places to anchor and places to be avoided. They would tell me when the best time to transverse a point was and areas that could be really nasty. These men and women made their livelihood on the sea and wanted to spare me some of the lessons they learned the hard way. I am grateful for the tremendous amount of help they gave me along the way.

During my stay at Eureka I was getting the chance to know the crews of one of the commercial fishing boats real well. That was the crew of the *Sisson Clipper*. Bud the captain, who also built the boat, his wife Patty, and two other girls, Betsy and Joanna, finished out the crew. I spent time with them almost every day. I was treated like family and my birthday was coming up, which would be my first birthday away from home. I am glad that I felt like I belonged. I am not sure why, but on birthdays and holidays I feel more alone than I do on other days. I know that one day is much like the day before it but on these special days when I wake up in the morning I just feel different. Maybe it is because birthdays and holidays are such a family-oriented time for me that I feel my family's absence most then.

I had been letting things slide for the past few days, and I decided that today was the day I had to get my act together. I had been putting off restocking the front cabin with canned goods for two reasons. One—I was lazy, and to restock the front cabin would mean crawling under the cockpit seat lockers from the aft cabin. I would have to pull out all the canned goods that would fit into the storage spaces in the front cabin and then rebalance the weight. So *Mary* would sit on her lines like she is supposed to. The main reason, though, is that I was afraid of what I would find. Sea water had come in through the bilge vents and drenched the cans in salt water. More than one person suggested that I shellac the cans, but all I could think of was the amount of work involved. Remember, I had a whole truckload of food on board. Now I had to pay the price for not taking the advice I was given. My diet would be controlled to some degree by what cans have to be used first. That is not that big of a problem right now because before I had to worry about what to make I would have to do the dishes. I did not have a clean cup, plate, or utensil aboard. I guess it must have been time for me to wash them.

I would take my first inland trip of the voyage while at Eureka. I was going to go to the redwood forest near Crescent City with the crew of the *Sisson Clipper*. The forest reminded me a lot of the woods in Washington. Only instead of giant Douglas fir trees they were giant redwoods. I took a lot of photos during my visit to the redwood forest. I thought that the law of averages meant that I would get at least a few good pictures out of the roll.

12.

EXTENDED FAMILY

I HAD BEEN at the dock now for five days and at four dollars and fifty cents a day, I had decided that it was time to anchor out. The lifestyle among the live-aboards at anchor in Eureka was much like every place else I would visit, that of a family. It was like being in a separate community and among friends. Everyone took turns cooking and eating on everyone else's boats, helping each other out and looking out for each other.

One of the inconvenient things about cruising is that when you are in port you are without transportation. I had a real funny thing happen to me one day that could have been very hard to explain. Milt, one of the live-aboards at the anchorage, offered me the use of his car, A VW bug, one day. Milt said it was in the lot near where we tied our skiffs when we went to town. "The key is under the mat," Milt said, but I was not sure which lot he meant. I found the bug near where we tied up our dinghies and sure enough, the key was under the floor mat. So here I was running all over town getting the things I needed before heading back to the boat. When I got back to the anchorage Milt asked if I used his bug today? I said yes, and thanks. He looked at me kind of strangely and said he never saw it leave. I asked him to describe the car and discovered that I had taken someone else's VW. Milt was still laughing as I was thinking how I could have explained this to the police if I had been pulled over for anything. I probably would still be in jail.

April twenty-third. It was my twenty-eighth birthday. It was also my first birthday away from home. I started my day out by diving for Milt to try to find an anchor he had lost during a winter storm. The only thing I found during the dive was an empty shell that I was told belonged to a moon snail, which is on the endangered species list. I did not feel very well after the dive so I puttered around the boat most of the day. I think I was feeling a little melancholy and lonely. I motored *Mary* to the new marina and did my laundry. That always signaled that I was thinking about my next port.

Earlier in the week I had been invited for dinner aboard the *Sisson Clipper*. The kindness and love they had shown me overwhelmed me. The dinner was great. The meal reminded me of the meals my mom made. It was a nice change from the meals I cook, although I was improving. After dinner I was given birthday presents, fishing gear. I must have been the only sailor who would starve if I had to live off the sea. They baked me a birthday cake and introduced me to a cute custom they have. They put coins, washers, dice, and anything else they can find, wrapped in aluminum foil, into the cake. It is like a surprise in every bite. After dinner, Loren from the yacht club dropped by and invited me to go to the old town pub with him. So I in turn invited Joanna and Betsy. This turned out to be one of the nicest birthdays I had ever had.

For the last two nights all of us in the anchorage had heard sharks thrashing about in the water during a feeding frenzy. It made me glad I was in *Mary* instead of in the water.

I was starting to feel like a regular tourist during my stay in port. I had been to the rhododendron parade, the park, the zoo, a mansion made from one redwood tree, a private club, and all the other points of interest Eureka had to offer.

I am not sure if everyone who cruises has the same amount of repairs to do that I had to do. Repairs require a lot of time! Both the repairs and the improvements I made helped to get *Mary* shipshape.

There are two other people I had the chance to meet during my stay in Eureka that I would like to mention. They are Mike and Laurie Phillips of the sailing vessel *Pnuma*. While I was at the anchorage I got the opportunity to go to church with them. I remember how excited Laurie was when she found out she was with child. She told me how she was going to fix up a berth for the baby and so on. The only time I went sailing while I was in port, Mike went with me. As a going-away present he gave me his coast pilot because I didn't have one.

In the days that I had been in port I had finally gotten *Mary* and more importantly myself prepared for whatever might lie ahead of us. Knowing that you are leaving port is both a sad and exciting time. It is exciting in that you are wondering what is waiting for you down the road. There is always a new adventure. The sad part about leaving port is that all the friends you have made since you came into port, some lasting friends, you have to say goodbye to. When you enter the next port you do not know anyone and the whole process starts over again and again and again. It is always the same.

13.
THE NIGHTMARE COMES TRUE

I LEFT EUREKA under full sail. I was hoping to try running under the 150% Genoa and the staysail if the wind was not too strong. I had heard of running under twin head sails and was hoping that I would get a break from the wheel. Sometimes things just do not go the way that you want them to. I did manage to get her to self-steer to some degree by balancing the helm.

Spring was beginning to transform into a California summer, and that would mean the arrival of fog, which plagues the coast this time of year. Within a few hours I had lost sight of land, and the fog surrounded me. A clearing in the fog that was not much bigger than *Mary* followed me or I should say surrounded me along the passage. At least I could see the water around my boat. The NOAA weather station said that the winds would be about fifteen knots and diminish towards evening. They lied again! The wind continued to build all day. I shorten more and more sail throughout the day until I was running under bare poles.

It is common knowledge that the best time to sail around a point is in the early morning or late evening. I did not know about this until I picked up the information from the commercial fishermen. The only problem is that during a passage you are bound to pass more than one point on any given run. The chances of crossing both at the optimum time are somewhere between slim and none. I passed the first point that day no problem, even though the weather conditions were worsening. The next point though was Point Agorta, and that was a different story. I was just across from the abandoned lighthouse when all hell broke loose. I was now in the middle of a confused mess of twenty-foot seas with spray flying everywhere. I felt like screaming, but even if I did, I would not have been able to hear myself over the fifty-knot wind that was screaming through the rigging. *Mary* was surfing at more than nine knots quite often and consistently was maintaining seven knots or more. I am not sure how other boats handle in conditions like this but as *Mary*'s speed increased over her hull speed the weather helm also increased. It was all I could do to maintain control surfing down these twenty-foot seas. There are two different schools of thought on how to sail in heavy weather. The one school states to heave to and ride it out or at least put out sea anchor to try to slow your speed down so you still have steerage. The second school of thought is the one I chose for a couple of reasons—to run with it. My biggest enemy during this passage was fatigue. So as long as I could control her I would be surfing much like the Beach Boys. In the back of my mind I knew that if I lost control just once it would be all over. With the momentum the boat had I would never be able to pull her out. It would be very easy to broach or pitch pole in the troughs of these giant waves. The chances of surviving that kind of disaster would be poor at best.

The wind caught the airfoil for my nonfunctioning wind vane and it flew off into the water. After very careful timing, I swung *Mary* around and after only two passes was able to retrieve it and had it lashed down. I was back on the original course running under a triple-reefed main alone. That is just a handkerchief of sail area to the wind for better stability. All of a sudden the steering went slack. I was thinking that the cable must have come off as it had on several other occasions. I was wrong. The force of the seas driving me must have been tremendous. When I looked at the rudder, the cables were still attached to the quadrant but a section of the rudder, more than four inches wide, had snapped off. A wave had snapped my rudder in half. Frantically I scrambled to attach the emergency tiller. I had never used the emergency tiller in conditions like this. I did not realize how much harder it would be to steer the boat. Not only was it twice as hard to steer *Mary* this way, the worst part was that I was now on the stern of the boat sitting on the rescue raft. I was squeezing the tiller with my hands and pushing my feet against the grab rails of the aft cabin. I was exposed to all the nasty stuff being thrown my way. The feeling was very much like a thrill ride at the fair. Only I could not get off. As the weather deteriorated more bad things happened. A wave came over the stern and broke the stainless bracket that holds one of the rescue rings and over it went. Trying to retrieve it was out of the question. My arms were aching from trying to hold *Mary* on a safe course. Another wave broke over me and slammed the boom into the Bimini top covering the cockpit, breaking it. For the first time in my life I did not think that I would make my next port. The dream that I had before leaving on this trip was coming true before my eyes. Now I understood what Curt meant when he said that the risks are too great. Right then, I agreed with him. A change in my spirit took place right then. I thought, if I can make San Francisco I will not have anything else to prove. Even if I have not demonstrated my skills and the seaworthiness of *Mary* to my critics, I will have proved it to myself, and that is all that matters. The exhaust coming from the engine looked different and I noticed that there was not any water coming out of it. *Mary* coming out of the water on these giant waves had allowed the water pump to lose its prime. I disconnected the intake hose and reconnected it in and the pump started to work again. With the coming of darkness and excitement of the day, I had missed a safe harbor, Shelter Cove.

I felt so cold. I was numb and exhausted beyond anything I had ever known. Even the fatigue of running a marathon does not compare with how I felt right then. I guess everyone has been without sleep for a few days, and knows that lightheaded feeling you get that reminds some people of being on drugs. The state of exhaustion I was feeling right then was far greater than that. As wiped out as I was, my mind was not working right. It seemed like it would be so easy to just drive the boat on the rocks and get off. It might not sound so crazy until you realize that there is no beach. This is a part of the coast where a sheer rock cliffs down to the water with nothing but more rocks down below. I was sure that it would mean certain death, but somehow I was not too concerned about it. The storm would not tire out and I had long since reached my limit. I did not know how I was still functioning even at this reduced rate. Somehow from the depths of myself there was a shred of sanity left, and I swung the tiller to starboard, to put some sea room between myself and this inhospitable rocky coast. At the last moment I had made the right decision.

The combination of the cold and my fatigue gave me the shakes. The kind that you cannot control. So here I was complaining to God about my problems. As soon as I had finished complaining, the wind changed. A warm Santa Ana wind, which came off the land, blew over me like the breath of God. Within a few hours I was warm again. As quickly as the storm had begun, she quieted back down, worn out from the anger she let loose, no doubt. So as she rested I heaved to and rested too.

At one in the morning I saw a fishing vessel and found out that I was twenty-three miles from Fort Bragg. When I reached sea buoy at Fort Bragg I radioed the Coast Guard to no avail. Any port can be dangerous at night, even more so if you are unfamiliar with the particular port. I had real difficulty reading the compass because during the storm a reef line from the main sail cut the power supply for the compass. I was lucky the line did not pull the compass off with it. It was now false dawn and I was piloting my way through the narrow channel. I saw several empty slips and I decided to try for the one at the end of the pier. All I could do was steer. The engine controls were in the center cockpit, and I was on the emergency tiller on the stern. I swung her close and ran over an aft cabin to cut power. I misjudged the speed and was just too slow. I hit the dock but was so tired that I didn't even care. I tied her securely and slept like a dead man, not even taking off my wet clothes. I woke up at eleven in the morning and reported my arrival to the harbor master. They charged me ten dollars a day mortgage. What a rip-off!

I felt driven by something to make repairs and leave the next day with the morning tide for San Francisco. It would have been a lot wiser to wait a few days to rest. I walked to town to eat and take a sauna. Somehow this combination revived me and I almost felt human. I called home and told them that I was all right. Back aboard I switched to the port fuel tank and went to sleep wondering what might lie ahead for me.

14.

STILL MORE CHALLENGES

BY SIX IN the morning I was making my way back to sea through the narrow channel. As soon as I cleared the channel leading to the open sea again I was met by eight- to ten-foot seas with a mild fifteen-knot wind. I was not going to take any chances that day. So before Point Arena, I reefed the main sail. I may never know why it was that the ocean was so rough around the points, but all hell broke loose again. The wind was suddenly a gale again and I was in fifteen-foot seas. There I was again under bare poles, but at least my steering worked, and I was not on the stern getting drowned by every breaking wave. The wind gradually eased up as I put some distance between myself and Point Arena. The wind stayed at about twenty five knots until dark. The radio was stating small craft warnings and fog warnings for the Bay Area. As darkness closed in so too did the fog. I decided to put into Bodega Bay and make the last thirty to forty miles to San Francisco Bay the next morning.

I remember the first time I was on the water at night. I was in a fourteen-foot runabout with a couple of friends. We had to go through a winding slough with log rafts all around to make it out into the Columbia River. As we were returning from this adventure one of my friends was holding the spotlight wires to the battery so I could see where I was going. At a crucial point in the maze of log rafts the light went dead. Before I knew what was happening we were on top of a log raft. We almost sank the boat when we slid her back into the water and with full power we could barely move. Boy was I glad to get it back on the trailer that night. My other experience at night was with *Mary* sailing around Fishers Island. It was a beautiful night out and I was not paying much attention to what I was doing. I turned around and looked up to see a bright star. Only the star was moving. An oil tanker was almost on top of me. Prior to the trip I was now on, that had been the extent of my night-time sailing experience. It is very different to run under instruments alone. I could not see much farther than the end of the boat so I had to put my trust in the electronics I had on board. The fathometer showed that I was getting in shallow water so I headed out to sea again, and rounded Bodega Head. By luck, I found the buoy right where the log and fathometer said it would be. I decided to heave to and look up in the Coast Pilot that Mike and Laurie Phillips had given me the course I should steer. I plotted the course and went for it. I felt a lot of pride when I dropped the anchor on entering a unfamiliar port in the dark and fog under the best navigation that I had done the entire trip. The seas never seemed to be mediocre. They were either great conditions or stormy. I had had my fill of storms! On the passage from Fort Bragg to here I had been soaked to the skin by seas breaking over the boat, the steering cable came off, which I easily put back on, and even with my fatigue this had been a lot easier sail than it was the day before. Time to sleep.

It was four in the afternoon and I had to leave this harbor. The fog was so thick that I could see less than a quarter of a mile. The wind was still howling, at thirty-five knots and changing direction to the west, according to the weather reports. The Coast Pilot said that Bodega Bay was not safe in a west wind. I never thought I would leave a port to sail into a storm but here I was doing exactly that. And to top it off it was Friday! Remember you do not want to leave port on Friday. I saw that some of the boats were already heading out to sea. They had radar or loran no doubt. I talked to a fishermen by radio, and he said that there were ten-foot seas and thirty-five knots of wind. Oh joy, here I go again. I had found that it was more pleasant to steer with my eyes closed, to steer just by feel. When I had my eyes opened I saw the waves being whipped by the wind, and towering over me like a mountain. I struggled in the troughs after surfing down these giant waves. It was more of a battle for me when I was distracted by these surroundings.

My navigation needed to be right or I would be in big trouble. I prayed for God to give me direction. The steering went slack again and I was back on the emergency tiller. I hated to have to steer this way. I decided to heave to and fix it. Every few minutes an occasional wave would drop by and visit me in the cockpit. Just a friendly visit, you see, and not nearly as damaging as the ones around Point Agorta. After a while it seemed I was not a participant at all, but just watching what was going on, like on television. This may have been because of emotional overload and was my mind's way of preserving sanity.

I spent a lot of time talking to the Lord. He was with me in all that I had been through.

At the San Francisco navigational buoy, I ran out of fuel in the port tank. There I was sitting in the troughs of ten-foot seas rolling from beam to beam watching everything on one side of the cabin change sides with everything on the other side. When a diesel engine runs out of fuel you have to bleed all the air out of the fuel lines or the engine will not work. This is a messy and smelly job that in seas like this can make even someone with an iron stomach queasy. After cut knuckles, and a lot of persuasion with strong language, the engine decided to work. It was either work or be thrown overboard.

It was the first of May as I passed under the Golden Gate Bridge. With stopping for repairs and sightseeing it had taken me more than a month to finally reach San Francisco Bay. I asked another vessel by radio where the best place to dock was and they told me Sausalito, so that is where I headed.

The difference between the open sea and the protection offered by the bay was hard to believe. The wind was probably about the same strength but the seas were only about two feet—what a difference wave height makes. If that surprised me, it was nothing compared to the difference I experienced between the open San Francisco Bay and Richardson Bay, where Sausalito is located. It was mind-boggling. San Francisco Bay was foggy and overcast and Sausalito was warm and had blue skies. When I tied up at Pelican Marina the change that began in me when I started on the trip was complete. I had gained the knowledge that I do not have to prove anything to anyone else again. I had lost my competitive drive, which is a fair exchange I would say. After calling home to say that I had made it safely I took a hot shower and treated myself to a steak dinner. All was right with the world again!

15.
SAUSALITO

ONE OF THE predominant features of the weather around San Francisco area in the summer is fog. Mark Twain once wrote that "the coldest winter he ever spent was a Summer in San Francisco." Yet there is a gem in the Bay Area that is exempt from this weather pattern. The rest of the bay will have fog and drizzle but this place will have warm blue skies and gentle breezes. The place I am talking about is Sausalito on Richardson's Bay. Maybe it is the mountains which protect Sausalito that contribute to its fine weather. Whatever it is, though I am grateful for it. Because of Sausalito's fine climate, many of the restaurants here have back courtyards with greenery everywhere. I even saw sidewalk seating for the first time at the Café Tries. Sausalito boasts of many fine restaurants and I had the opportunity to dine at many of them. Since Sausalito is a seaport town, you will find several seafood restaurants, as well as just about every other kind of food you crave. One place I want to mention is Zack's. The food was just average but the entertainment was something else. The entertainment I am referring to was not the wild rock bands, though that was a show in itself, but the races. What kind of races you ask? Well turtle races on the dock outside. There were circles painted on the deck and the starting gate was, what else, a wash tub. The first turtle across the painted rings wins. They started with turtles that were about two inches across, and they got bigger with each succeeding race until the last race featured turtles that were more than a foot across. People in the audience were picked to sponsor a turtle and if their turtle won, they received a Zack's T-shirt with the likeness of a turtle on it.

Cities seem so cold and impersonal to me after sailing alone. Six people seem like a crowd. After a few hours with all the people crowding me I felt like I had to be alone. Sausalito reminded me more of a European village. Maybe it was the informal friendly atmosphere, or the many artists who live in the area. Sausalito is one of my favorite places.

Sausalito has much to offer. There are curio shops, art galleries, and for those who want to burn off some of the calories from the great meals, dancing. The quality of the music is far better than what my home town has to offer. Sausalito is a mixture of several different cultures, which is evident in the variety of the music you will hear. I went out on the town one night and heard jazz, rock, and Italian folk music. You can spend every evening listening to a different kind of music and relaxing, the latter being a prime occupation of those who cruise while they are in port.

I think the pace is slower here than in most cities. This is a tourist town, but unusual as it might seem, everyone is friendly. Some of the nicest people I have ever had the pleasure to meet are at the Sausalito cruising club. They really rolled out the welcome mat for me. I had full use of the club, including the hot showers, what a lovely phrase, hot showers. I was treated like family, maybe better. I was made to feel special. They have a bring-your-own-meat barbecue and provide all the trimmings for a nominal fee. Special kindness was extended to me by Barbara and Howard

Mackie. I hope someday I will be able to help a stranger the way that they helped me.

If you like flowers and shrubs you will be in awe of all the beauty lining the streets. The overall effect is a park-like setting and not just cold impersonal concrete. In fact, there are several fruit trees whose fruit is free for the taking. As I walked down the tree-lined streets, which all seemed to lead to the waterfront, I discovered that the waterfront was indeed the heart of activity here. I could see more classic wooden vessels here than anyplace else on the Pacific coast. Many of them compete in the famous master mariners race each year.

I am sure many a dream has been inspired by walking these docks and being captured by the beauty whose masts touch the sky. There are so many exceptional vessels here that the outstanding seems commonplace. You just can not appreciate them as you would if you saw just one at a time. Because San Francisco is a hopping-off point for the west as well as north and south, I saw vessels from around the world with their names painted proudly on their sterns. Sausalito is an excellent port for the transient vessel because needed supplies are within walking distance, and if needed, the Golden Gate transit system has buses that go all over. One note of caution: make sure you have correct change. The only time I was treated rudely was when I only had a twenty-dollar bill and did not have correct change for the fare.

A little side trip while you are at Sausalito that should not be missed is a sail to Angel Island. Hospital Cove is an excellent place to land and has mooring buoys you tie to bow and stern. There is a tram that will take you to the top of the island or you can walk as I have. On a clear day the view from the top is worth the effort of the walk. I could see all the Bay Area because this is one of the highest places in San Francisco Bay. While I was there the island deer would come up and eat out of my hand. The park has provided picnic tables which are nestled among the palm trees that have been planted over the years. It was a treat for me, because there are very few palms in the Pacific Northwest. I really enjoyed my stay at what must be one of California's most beautiful parks.

16.

LIFE ON THE HOOK

THE BUDGET-MINDED CRUISER can stay free in the designated general anchorages at Sausalito. You are likely to see almost anything there. For instance there is a floating island we named Gilligan's Island. It has fake palm trees on it and the entrance is a cave with living quarters below water. There is a glistening white palace which we call the Taj Mahal at the other end of the spectrum and everything in between. The lifestyle of being on the hook is far different from staying at a dock. When you are staying at a dock, at least for me, your boat is just a place for you to sleep. You are still dependent on land for power, water, etc. You might get to know some of the owners of boats berthed close to you but generally you are no closer to them than the neighbors you would have on land. Being on the hook is a much different lifestyle. Think of this. You have no electric bill, no water bill, no phone bill, or even rent or house payment. The only real expense you have is the food you eat. On top of that most people on the hook do not have regular jobs that they have to report to each day. You go to bed when you are tired and wake up when the sun shines through the hatch in the morning. There is also a tremendous sense of independence while on the hook because if you do not like your surroundings or your neighbors you can simply pull up your anchor and go to a place that suits your liking better. I think that the best way to describe what the community on the hook is like is to give you a few examples of the boats and their crews.

The first vessel is the *Brigadoon*, a twenty-four-foot fiberglass sloop. Her master Jack, a retired Merchant Marine, plans another trip to Mexico. He is a good friend and sailing partner. His first mate is a cantankerous cat. When Jack talks on his ham radio the cat bites him. When he is sleeping, the cat bites him. If he watches TV, the cat bites him. Do you see a pattern here? I think the first mate wants the Captain's complete attention.

Then there is the *Paramore*, a thirty-foot ketch. The Captain is Tim and his first mate, Tina. Like almost everyone who is anchored out they also dream of cruising. They are also semi-retired, even though they are in their mid-thirties. It does not take much to live anchored out. You do not pay rent, telephone or any of the other things we just cannot do without on land. There is a thirty-foot trimaran with Bob and his wife Janet aboard. They have done some cruising and are working towards future goals. Lee of the *Typhoon*, a forty-four-foot ketch, is quite a character. The last time he shaved was probably fifteen years ago. The result is a magnificent beard long enough to tie behind his back. He is a shipwright by trade and a perfectionist. We share many a meal.

We also have a celebrity in our anchorage—Bernard Moitessier aboard his forty-foot red-hulled vessel *Joshua*. Bernard is one of the most famous sailors in the world. He is a published author, having written many books about sailing, one of his most successful called *The Long Way*. This book is his story about the first Golden Globe single-handed around-the-world race back in 1968, which he won. During my time here I have the opportunity to get to know this gentle quiet man.

Every community has those who are on the fringe of their

society and the last boat and crew fit this pattern. The best way I can describe them is to compare them to modern-day pirates. This last vessel in our community on the hook is a vessel whose name I can not mention. She is a fifty-four-foot gaff-rigged schooner with a hired skipper whom I also can not name. The owner, an artist, is rarely around and the hired skipper whom I cannot name treated her as his own. His adventures alone could fill many books. An example of one of them is a time we all went to get bottom paint for our boats at a surplus store. The salesman was really kind to us. We were all laughing and having a good time when I could not believe what I saw. Somehow a case of gray paint and a case of orange juice had made their way into the van. I was angry and ashamed that the skipper whom I shall not name and his crew had taken those things. Another time, the skipper whom I shall not name and one of his female guests decided it was shower time and bathed right on deck in front of God and everyone. And this does not even include the wild parties aboard the vessel whose name I can not mention.

The community of boaters on the hook has advantages over their brothers on land. Everyone takes turn eating on the different boats and if anyone needs help, like when Tim and Tina refinished their boat, everyone pitches right in. I think it is more like the frontier days when everyone pitched in to build each other's houses. The lifestyle is much more laid back because in general, they do not have the cares or worries that go along with terra firma.

17.

GUESTS ARRIVE

AFTER I HAD spent more than a month alone Dave Rockwood was going to spend two weeks with me. It was a nice surprise. I was looking forward to seeing him and having someone to share the experience of cruising the Delta. I received a message that someone was trying to reach me by radio telephone. Since I did not have the channels on my radio that they were using here I had to find another vessel that did. I walked back to Pelican Marina and saw another owner working on his North Sea twenty-seven. I was able to make the connection with the people who were trying to get a hold of me by radio telephone. No sooner had I finished talking with them, Mike and Joan Wey, who would be there on Wednesday, than I saw Dave walk by. It looked like I would have a full house on the boat for a while.

I motored *Mary* to Pelican Marina to pick up Dave's stuff. I could not believe everything he had. He brought a bowling ball, guitar, schoolbooks, and enough clothes to last someone cruising for a year. In other words, he made the same mistakes we all make our first time.

The front cabin was twice as big as the aft cabin but there was not much room to sit down once all the gear was loaded. I had a yacht broker look at *Mary* today and he said it was hard to tell with all the stuff inside but thought she should be worth twenty-five thousand dollars.

I have seen the Bay Area by boat, and now I would get the chance to see it as a tourist by car. Dave had all of our time planned out for things he wanted to see, so it is off to Golden Gate Park, Fisherman's Wharf, and a movie.

The next few days went by fast. I was spending a lot more on groceries for four of us than I would have for myself, but in a short time I would be alone again, and would not be spending anything. The last three days would become some of my fondest memories.

Mike and Joan arrived on Wednesday, their tenth anniversary, and we went for a beautiful sail around the bay and came to rest in Hospital Cove on Angel Island. Another sailor, a Christian man, assisted us on tying up to the mooring buoys. What a gorgeous spring day—bright sunshine, green grass, and palm trees. The temptation was too great and we decided to have a picnic ashore. The scent of all the flowers, and just being in the company of friends, made me glad to be alive. There were deer that came up and ate out of our hands on the island. We had a nice dinner aboard and opened the champagne Mike and Joan gave me when I left on the trip. Joan is giggling after a few glasses.

We decided to sneak back on the island. I say sneak because the park closes at sunset. We enjoyed the view from the top of the island where Dave and I had walked earlier in the day. The sight commands a panoramic view of the entire Bay Area, and surprise surprise, no fog tonight. Everything was lit up, and we could pick out the different landmarks such as Ghirardelli Square, the Transamerica building, and many others. It was one of the prettiest sights at night that I have ever seen, and well worth the climb. We overloaded *Skipper*, which is the name of the dinghy, and once again rowed back to *Mary*, for a good night's sleep. The next day we would all go and share the sights of San Francisco.

None of us got up very early and were just enjoying not having to rush. We took some pictures of seagulls and ducks fighting over scraps from our lunch. We discovered that they do not like radishes. We sailed back to the marina to get cleaned up and see the town. Joan had a nice dress on, and my suit, which had fit when I left, was about two sizes too big for me. I would have Dave take it home when he leaves. We took in the sights of Fisherman's Wharf at night including dinner in a restaurant with a medieval atmosphere. When the next day arrived, we were off to see Golden Gate Park. There was never enough time to see all the things you want to see when you are on a time schedule. We did get a chance to see the museum, aquarium, and planetarium before hitting Fisherman's Wharf for souvenirs. Then we had to rush to make the train that would take Mike and Joan home.

How am I going to feel when everyone leaves? I am concerned about leaving *Mary* anchored alone for the week while David and I will be going inland.

We loaded up Dave's car with all the stuff for our inland cruise including the now-deflated dinghy. We were off to Magic Mountain. One of the things I had missed was the pleasure of a Big Mac, so I really indulged my craving when I had the chance. When we entered Magic Mountain we went on a lot of neat rides and decided to see a performance called magic moments in Hollywood. Well this turned out to be a Young Life crusade. I guess the Lord knows what I need. I discovered something that day that I had never realized before. The girls that I am attracted to have an innocence and purity about them. I think that it is their inner beauty that is shining through to the outside. We hit McDonald's one more time and then found a hotel for the night. It cost twenty-seven dollars and it was my turn to pay. I had become spoiled because it does not cost anything to stay on *Mary*—it is free. Tomorrow would bring Disneyland.

Disneyland was nice but it had lost some of the magic it held for me the first time I was there. I called Mom and wished her a happy Mother's Day. I thought I was starting to get on Dave's nerves a little but he never said anything. Tomorrow we would see the Hearst Castle. A change of menu today, A&W instead of McDonald's.

On the way from the Hearst Castle to Reno the car broke down. After a major hassle, we had her fixed but almost no money. I had left most of my money and my bank card on the boat. Not the smartest thing to do I would say. When we get to Carson City I wired for money.

Our next stop was Sparks to see the Harris Car Museum. We got to see Herbie the Love Bug. At 1 p.m. we went back to the bank and there was still no money. After several calls I got my Master Card number and thought, no problem. The number kept coming up invalid. It looked like we would have to try again tomorrow. We drove to Reno and gambled the huge sum of three dollars on the nickel machine. You might guess that we are not gamblers. After a few minutes we were flat broke. We sat around, read, and looked at the girls in short skirts. At midnight we decided to drive back to Carson City, and I nearly froze sleeping in the car. The head and neck cramps that I had in the morning could not be described. I did not get dinner last night or breakfast today, and my hunger only adds to my anger at the incompetence of the bank people back home. I would not have been so upset, except that I had made prior arrangements so if I got short on funds they would get me money in a hurry. It had been three days now and this is not what I would call fast service. After several more calls I discovered that one of my banks sent the money to the wrong bank and the other had not given me all the card numbers I needed. I could not remember when I had been so angry. More phone calls and I finally had money and we were on our way to Reno again. This time we were fed and I was feeling at least tolerable with the rest of the world. Jan and Dean were playing at Reno that night but with all that had happened I did not feel like spending another day away from the peace of *Mary*. We headed back to Sausalito.

After driving all night we were back to where *Mary* should have been anchored. But no *Mary*. After searching the area, I saw her about a quarter of a mile from where she had been. She must have dragged anchor. The pump for the dinghy was not working right, but I managed to get the dinghy inflated enough to row out to the boat. After being abandoned for five days she was still dry. That is a relief! Dave said he was going home the next day. While I was away from *Mary* I worried about her and could not wait to head on south but now I felt a loneliness that left me drained. I was really glad that Dave, Joan, and Mike came down to see me but I knew the loneliness would be many times greater when they had gone. I just did not know what to do. I remembered the saying, "It knocked the wind out of my sails." That was how I felt right then, just drifting. I did my laundry for the first time since Eureka, and I would have Dave take back some of my stuff for me. I felt that I was starting to grown patience, but this is only the first step of the long journey into becoming the person I hope to be.

Every time I saaw little children playing I thought of Tashera and how much I missed her and I wondered what direction my life was going. I had a lot of letters to write that night before Dave left the next day. I wanted to touch base with my friends and family back home and Dave had promised to deliver the letters for me. My mind was consumed with one thought, when Dave leaves, what will I do then?

After Dave left, I feel like screaming I am alone! I woke up to discover that *Skipper*, my dinghy, was upside down. I had left the dinghy in the water last night and the high winds flipped her over. I lost the oars, the pump, and the bag she was stored in on deck. It was safe to say my day was not starting out real well. My spirit was really low and the loneliness enveloped me once more.

I have discovered that when I am discouraged and aimless,

having a goal or direction for my life sets things in their proper perspective. I had wanted to go to the Delta with Dave so I would have someone to share the adventure with but things just did not work out that way. I had heard so much about the place and it was so close, only a day or two away, I decided to go and spend the week exploring and resting.

The first thing on the agenda was to replace all the stuff I lost from the dinghy. What a shock. The items I had to replace cost forty-eight dollars and that was for the cheap kind. If I had replaced the exact items that were lost the bill would have been more than one hundred dollars. During the past few days I had gotten to know several other cruisers in this anchorage. I was blessed to be able to call them friends. Their fellowship eased the aches of loneliness.

I had not slept well the last few nights because of the high winds. So when the weather cleared I deserved the luxury of sleeping in. I do not know if you have ever been frightened awake before, but I was today. I felt a hard crash and jumped on deck in my underwear to see this two-story houseboat towering over me. I surveyed the damage left in the houseboat's wake after hitting me. The bowsprit was raised half an inch and the stem had a crack in it. The starboard side of my hull was also damaged from the collision. I do not think I can describe the anger that was overcoming me at that moment. All I knew was that the owner was going to pay for the damages or pay the consequences. I felt like the song that said, "if it weren't for bad luck I would have no luck at all."

I needed to turn in early that night because I was going to run in the Bay to Breakers race in the morning. When you are used to not setting an alarm clock and waking up naturally every morning, having to get up at five-thirty in the morning came pretty early. I had to catch an early bus to San Francisco for the race so there I was up at the crack of dawn. I could not believe all the people that I see. The announcer at the start of the race informed us that there were forty thousand runners competing that day. It was hard to describe the scene. There were people everywhere.

The first three or four miles of the race were more like a walk than a run. It is no wonder it took me an hour to run 7.63 miles. It was reported that Craig Virgin won the race, which had more of a carnival atmosphere about it than the competitive races I had run in the past. There were people roped together that they called centipedes. I ran next to one of those centipedes, which was comprised of a bride, groom, and their wedding party. I had the chance to visit as we ran and was informed that the reception would be taking place at the finish line. After I finished the race I waited two hours to catch a bus back to where the race started but the line never seemed to move. I decided to walk the ten miles it was to the Golden Gate Bridge so I could catch a bus back to Sausalito. I could not wait to get back to *Mary*. I called Mom and was told that my brother Bob ran a race today too and that he took third place. He did a little better than I did I would say.

18.

THE DELTA

THE DELTA, OR more accurately the San Joaquin River Delta, has hundreds of miles of navigable water with great fishing, swimming, and relaxation.

As I made preparations so I could sail to the Delta I found that the days seemed to blend into one another. During the two weeks since Dave had left I had made *Mary* ready for another adventure. I raised the anchor and set sail for the Delta. From San Francisco Bay I sailed through San Pablo Bay to Suisun Bay and continued up to the protected waters of the Delta. I had been sailing for twelve hours, and was not too excited about the idea of sailing at night. I spotted a yacht basin and sneaked in and tied to the nearest slip. I hoped that I could get by without having to pay for moorage for the night. I got an early start by waking up at seven in the morning and took off for Mandeville. I got lucky and did not have to pay for moorage. As the sun got warmer I worked on my all-over tan. In the afternoon a gust of wind caused the main sail to jibe. Remember that is something that you do not want to do because bad things can happen and did. The main sheet caught the airfoil for the wind vane and flung it overboard. I turned around just in time to watch it sink out of sight. It was no great loss because it did not work very well anyway. By late afternoon I had the anchor down and a stern line tied to a tree. I was happier now than I had been in a long time! I had finally found peace.

My surroundings reminded me of pictures I had seen of the Florida Everglades. My senses were filled with the earthy smells and all the beauty surrounding me. I might stay there a week. My week turned into a month and in looking back over my life, if I had to pick one time when I was the happiest and most at peace, without a doubt it would be these weeks. I felt like I was in the Garden of Eden and the only thing missing in my life is my Eve. I felt that I was living more like God intended when he gave us life. When it got dark I went to sleep listening to the sounds of nature. There was never a schedule to keep and I never set an alarm. I woke usually when the sun was shining through the hatch in the morning. I ate when I was hungry and did not have to worry about work or even time for that matter. Time took on an entirely different meaning now. Back home time was almost an enemy you tried to beat. I was always trying to manage time, to squeeze more into each day. I had discovered that living that way robs you of peace in your life. The more you try to do the lesser the quality of life you have.

I realized that you cannot manipulate time, and that time was not my enemy. I discovered that time was much like the river all around me, it just flows. My days sailing the Delta allowed me to mend *Mary* from the damage she had incurred during the trip. Something special was taking place at the same time. My spirit was being mended and I was able to reflect on the various elements of my life and accept the things in my life that I could not change. **I had found the peace that I was searching for, and it was inside me all the time.**

Each day was new and alive and every place I visited gave

me more than its share of good memories. From swimming every day in the seventy-two degree water, to waterskiing with friends I made who had powerboats, to watching the raccoons come for food in the evening. There were wild blackberries on the islands and butterflies everywhere. I took two rolls of film from my journey throughout the Delta hoping for pictures to remind me of this special time. There is an art to taking good pictures. I have never had much success taking pictures of wild life. The animals never seemed to stand still and say cheese for me. By the time I could get the camera focused they were usually gone. In the evenings the crickets sang me to sleep and the sunsets were too spectacular to describe. The colors were something you would have to see to believe. The Delta was the first place where I was actually able to buddy boat. While cruising in the Meadows and Lost Slough it was days before we saw another living soul. Besides the company, one of the great things about buddy boating was the shared meals, which were a welcome relief from my own cooking. The wonderful weather was allowing me to sleep in the cockpit under the stars.

I had really been blessed with all the friends I had made on this part of my journey, but I had decided that my next adventure would be to sail to the Channel Islands off Southern California. After this last adventure I would then go home to those I love. More and more my thoughts are back were my heart is.

I wanted to make the sail back to Sausalito in one day so I got up really early to sail past landmarks that now had much more meaning to me. There was the beached ferry, which now housed a farmer's goats, past the moth-balled Navy fleet, and other special places too numerous to mention back to my anchorage at Sausalito. My home away from home.

19.

HOME AWAY FROM HOME

MY FIRST DAY back at Sausalito was a mixture of good and bad. It was great to see all my friends in port and a special surprise to see Steve Dahlgren, his wife, and their twin two-year-old boys who had just arrived at the anchorage. I first met Steve and his family in Eureka, California. He was one of the first people I met in that port and he was kind to me. That had extra meaning now that I was sailing alone. My bad experience came as a result of the crew of the vessel whose name I can not mention. Their skipper who shall not be named was getting ready to sail to Monterey and he had assembled a motley crew together. As usual they were raising hell in our normally quiet anchorage. They were water ballooning the boats in the anchorage and one of their bombs made it through my open hatch. The water balloons did not bother me as much as the ones that were filled with shaving cream. Those were a mess to clean up. I was really angry and if they did it again I would leave port. I did not have to put up with this.

One of the things that added to my feeling of independence while I was cruising was if I liked the people in the anchorage I could stay as long as I wanted. If on the other hand you do not like the attitude of the people where you are, you simply lift your anchor and move to a friendlier climate.

As always, my plan was to just stay in port a day and it turned into a week. I would not go offshore unprepared. I put a pretty high price of my life and I think that is one of the reasons I did not want to buddy boat to Monterey with the vessel I cannot name. They had no engine, no radio, no bilge pump, and their boat is leaking from rot in the keelson. Their boat was an accident waiting to happen. I also had other bad experiences involving the vessel I cannot name while at anchor. They borrowed tools and broke them. The skipper I cannot name offered me a crappy tool to make it up to me but I am still out the money to replace tools that I need. I do not want to babysit them down the coast or support their cruising.

The next few days found me buying supplies and making improvements to *Mary*. A nice thing that happened on one of my buying trips was running into Bert and Jodi, whom I had met in the Delta. It was good to see them again and they offered me a ride and help with my supplies. The day was topped off by a great evening sail on *Mary* with Lee as first mate. There was not a lot of wind but we had enough maneuverability to do anything we wanted to do. It was great to go all through the anchorage circling the boats of friends. In fact Lee was able to board his own boat from mine while I was under sail. I just came alongside and he stepped off. I swung the wheel over and headed back to my little spot and dropped the hook. As I furled the sails the sun was just dropping below the mountains, the end to a perfect day.

The next evening the vessel I cannot name was leaving port and Jack, Lee, and I decided to sail as far as San Francisco Bay with them. I had the stove fired up so we were feasting on spam and pineapple with corn and fresh vegetables while under way. Just outside of Richardson Bay, we saw that the vessel I cannot name is fending off the Spinnaker Restaurant with oars. We threw them a line and towed them free. Maybe you can see why I did not want to buddy boat down the coast with them. I get tired enough at sea just taking care of myself. The next day I would be busy as last days in port always were. I visited with Bernard Moitessier today and Walt Piro and took a pamphlet describing their adventures. I made the normal calls to home I always made before leaving port. One call I made was to Joan Wey. She was insistent that I should not go offshore again because of the dream she had. The next call I made was even more painful. As I told Mom that I was ready to leave port she related an event that took place the other day. Tashera, my daughter, and Jennifer, my niece, were spending the day at Mom and Dad's house. My mom said, "Here comes daddy," and the kids ran to the door. When they came back, Jennifer was with her dad Scott and Tashera had big tears running down her face and she said, "That's not my daddy." Hearing her tell the story broke my heart. I did not know what to do. The situation had not changed at home, and I would still have hassles every time I wanted to see Tashera. After the divorce the court decided when I could see my daughter but there always seemed to be some reason why she was not allowed to go. It was a no-win situation and we both ended up losing. I wanted to be with her, but to do that, I would have to sail a thousand miles back up the coast against headwinds and unfriendly seas. Sometimes life deals you a rotten hand but you have to play the game to its conclusion.

20.
SOUTHERN CALIFORNIA

IT WAS NOW the 22nd of June and I had been living this adventure for more than four months. I did not sleep well last night because my mind was going over everything that I had to do to make sure I was ready to go offshore. One of the points of Murphy's Law says that "anything that can go wrong, will go wrong at the most inopportune time." So I tried to lessen those chances. After goodbyes to friends, I pulled the anchor and set sail for Monterey.

What an exhausting trip to Monterey. Because of the ten-foot seas I could not get *Mary* to self steer, and the fluky winds made me change sails more times than I care to remember. That, coupled with twenty-three hours at the wheel, almost did me in.

I was surprised when I entered port that the vessel I cannot name was not in sight. I asked the port captain; he said she was reported overdue. The news made me sad. I later found out that she had put into Santa Cruz. It took them twice the time it took me to cover the same distance.

I hated having to sail under a time schedule. I delayed leaving Sausalito so long that I did not know if I would be able to meet

Tom Lowe at Santa Barbara on time. So with less than sixteen hours in port I started the run to Santa Barbara. I was hoping to be able to stay awake for the thirty hours I thought it would take me to reach Santa Barbara but my luck just would not last. Somehow a fuse blew and the electric fuel pump went out. That meant I had to once again bleed the entire fuel system before the engine would work.

I decided to stop at San Luis Obispo to anchor at seven-thirty in the morning to sleep a few hours before being back at sea by two-thirty in the afternoon. By eleven at night I was near Point Arguello sailing through the darkest night I had ever seen. The darkness should have given me a clue as to what lay ahead. By the time I reached Point Conception I was sailing in a whole gale once again. There were more seas breaking over the boat and into the cockpit that night than ever before. Not only was I drenched, but a wave also soaked my charts, and the radio direction finder. To top that off the VHF radio was on the blink and not working. I could not call for help if I wanted to. It took me seven hours to make twelve miles headway through this mess. Somehow during the night I lost twenty miles. On the horizon I saw a light where I thought shore should be. After hours of fighting my way towards it, I discovered it was an oil rig, which dwarfed my boat. It was like a dream, a floating city that did not appear on my charts. I changed course once again, and by this time Point Conception was now ten miles astern. The wind and seas had died down. The fear for my life I felt during the storm had also subsided. The word I used to describe the passage in my log book is unprintable. I saw a sailboat in the distance and raised him by radio. He was a delivery captain who was making the passage from Taiwan to San Diego. The captain said we would make Santa Barbara by the afternoon. This passage had been some of the worst for weather conditions, but had been the best by far in the rich marine life I have seen.

Off of Monterey I got within sixty feet of a gray whale. After

I took several pictures I started to think that it might not be too safe sailing so close to the whale. I altered course one direction and the whale altered course the opposite direction. He must have been thinking the same thing I was.

I was surprised that I have not seen the birds offshore that I was used to seeing at the beaches. I saw birds that looked like penguins with their little white tuxedo shirts on. As I sailed within a few feet of them, some would dive underwater and others would fly away or I should say try to fly away. They were really terrible flyers. Most of the time they would use their wings like flippers to move out of the way. It did not dawn on me that they were not penguins until I saw them fly. Pretty dumb huh. I also got the chance to see hundreds of pelicans. They were beautiful to see gliding just above the waves.

I am really disappointed that man has almost extinguished the sea otter. I saw one at Monterey, but that is the only place. I remember reading that there were thousands of them and now they are almost gone. I do not know if the oil wells are responsible or not. I do know that when I cleared Point Conception and entered Southern California there was oil all over on the water. The tragic thought I had is that many of the things I had seen on this trip would not be here in the future if people do not change. When the last of a species is gone you will not be able to bring it back. It seems that during every passage, things have a way of balancing each other out. The richness of marine life balanced out the severity of the storms from San Francisco to Santa Barbara.

21.

THE CHANNEL ISLANDS

WHEN I CLEARED the breakwater at Santa Barbara I saw Tom standing with his baggage waiting for my arrival. The first thing we did after getting a berth was to take all the cushions out of the boat and lay them in the sun on the dock to dry. You can usually tell who has just entered port by the amount of clothes and other gear they have drying in the sun. Invariably someone would come by and ask if my boat leaks. What a question. I do not think any boat is dry when waves are breaking over it, soaking your gear through open hatches.

After we had the boat put back together Tom treated me to a fine dinner. I think any dinner you do not have to cook or clean up after is fine! After dinner, we went to a movie, *Raiders of the Lost Ark*. Had it been any other movie I do not think I would have been able to stay awake. Then finally the comfort of a warm, dry bed.

Tom restocked our provisions while I was sleeping. I rolled out of bed at one in the afternoon and we walked to the waterfront and rented diving gear for Tom. By two in the afternoon, we were ready to set sail for Santa Cruz Island. The wind died down enough so we could sail under Main and 150 Genoa. I could not believe the difference calm seas made. There was still some slop left over from the gale I came in on, but it was calm enough that I could balance the helm and *Mary* was self steering all the way to Santa Cruz Island at five to six knots. We anchored in our own little cove, but the groundswell was so bad, we raised the anchor and moved to another location where two other sailboats were. I was reading *Two Years Before the Mast*, and I was seeing the same places Dana was writing about over one hundred years ago. He commented about the terrible groundswell at Santa Barbara, and now I understood why!

Tom and I explored a cave today in *Skipper*. It was an eerie feeling as we rowed into the cave. We saw starfish on the walls and heard the rushing of water running through paths it has carved in the rocks. We did not bring a flashlight so after a few feet we were enveloped in darkness. Tom snapped a few flash pictures and said, "Okay, let's go back." I was also a little apprehensive about spending too much time in the cave. If the tide came in we could get trapped inside. It was still cool to explore the cave and more importantly have someone to share the experience with.

We explored this section of the island by landing our dinghy in another cave that had an opening to the land. We found after a while that this was a lot drier than trying to land through the surf. The island was pretty barren, with the only trees being in the valleys. The rest of the island was dry and brown and uninviting, with cliffs surrounding most of the island. We hiked up one of the valleys and found a waterfall. Tom took pictures of me in front of it. We went beachcombing and found some shells on the rocky beach that we added to our collection.

Tom was used to a faster paced life and was anxious to move on in the morning so we rowed back to *Mary* for a relaxing evening. We sailed for twenty miles today and several boats were at anchor. We found out that people aboard were diving for abalone.

I was invited to go along for the dive but I did not feel up to it. As evening descended almost everyone else left the anchorage. I was not feeling very well so I went to bed early. Tom had been quiet since we left Santa Barbara. In the middle of the night he woke me up to say he wanted to go back to the mainland now! I told him that there was no way I was going to leave and enter port at night. I told him that if he woke me by a certain time I would plot the course back to Santa Barbara. So in the early morning we raised sail and headed back to Santa Barbara, or so I thought. When we reached the mainland, I did not know where we were. That meant we were south of Santa Barbara. I thought it was no big deal, I would just start the engine and we would motor up the coast to Santa Barbara. Well, Murphy's Law was holding true. The engine would not start. I tried everything I could think of to coax it to start without success. So Tom and I talked it over and headed south for Ventura, the closest southern point.

By late afternoon, the wind was picking up strength and I could not reach the harbor master for instructions on the VHF radio. The radio was out of commission again and once we committed ourselves to go through the narrow channel there would be no turning back. We would have to live with our decision. A major problem is that we did not know which entrance we were supposed to go in. We kept one eye on the depth gauge as the numbers got smaller and smaller. The gauge registered four feet and we draw three and one-half feet. The harbor patrol met us when we cleared the breakwater and towed us to a slip. He said he saw us coming in and thought for sure he would have to tow us off the sandbar. We came in through the sand trap entrance instead of the main entrance. We had at least some good luck today. The moorage was ten dollars a night and Tom had had his fill of sailing. He was ready to leave me to visit friends in San Diego. I did not blame him, though; this is not what I would call a great vacation for him.

I enjoyed the best meal I had ever had at a restaurant that

night overlooking the boats at the marina. The next night Tom and I ate at a Mexican restaurant with pictures on the wall of movie stars who had eaten there. The food was good and reasonably priced. There were so many beautiful houses at Ventura. Seeing them and their beautiful, landscaped yards is what I envision when I hear people talking about living the great American dream. I had a mechanic work on *Mary* and he stated that she was fixed so Tom left for San Diego.

22. BEATING UP THE COAST

AFTER TOM LEFT I window-shopped at the stores on the waterfront. At a bookstore I saw an advertisement for the movie *The Long Way* by Bernard Moitessier that would be shown at Santa Barbara the next evening. I decided to beat back up the coast to Santa Barbara and say hi to someone from my home away from home, Sausalito.

My trip up the coast was slow, but otherwise uneventful. I saw Ann and David at the show and was honored by all the attention Bernard gave me during the showing. His recognition made me feel important. I thought I had gained some type of reputation in the San Francisco area because I survived sailing alone down the coast at the wrong time of year.

The next several days I spent anchored at Santa Barbara with the only major event being tossed into the water when the dinghy was flipped over in the surf. Ann, David, and I met to see Tristan Jones, another accomplished author and sailor, give a presentation. When I was ready to row back to *Mary* that night it took me two tries to make it through the surf. I was successful only by walking *Skipper* out through the surf till I was up to my neck in the water, pulling myself in the dinghy and rowing like mad. Barbara, another friend, would visit soon. I sure hoped I could talk Barbara into sailing back up to San Francisco with me when she arrived for her two-week vacation. I only had one hundred dollars left and I hoped that that was enough money to get me home.

The Fourth of July found me anchored outside the surf line at Santa Barbara. As I watched the families setting off fireworks on the beach I was wondering what my family was doing back home. I was sure they would be watching the fireworks at Lake Sacajawea, the culmination of all the different activities that take place during the day. I found my thoughts were turning more and more towards home.

Maintenance continued to occupy a lot of my time. I made a point of wetting the deck and especially the cabin top daily because of all the checking that was appearing recently. The checking was caused from the wood drying out in the hot sun. The rest of the time I relaxed and read. I had read virtually all the books my brother Bob sent with me. Sitting here at anchor was unbearable. Tropical Storm Beatrice was about six hundred miles away and moving towards me. The rolling in the anchorage rocked me from beam to beam until I can not stand it anymore.

One night I left the anchorage under sail because the engine would not start of course. The motion was more bearable under sail than just rolling back and forth in the troughs. I did not have my contacts in so I could not see very well. *Mary* became fouled on the stern line of *Dark Star*. It is a good thing because I probably would have hit her if I had not. After anxious minutes I managed to pull myself off the other boat's stern line. I set course for Santa Cruz Island and went to sleep. That was pretty foolish because it would mean crossing two shipping lanes during the night. My fatigue was greater than my wisdom.

I spent the next day in one of the prettiest coves on Santa Cruz Island, that being Smugglers Cove. From where I was anchored I could see a grove of trees and in the distance Anacorpa Island. During the day three other sailboats came into this quiet cove. They were all ketches so my boat was the only single-masted boat in the cove. The anchorage continued to fill up as the sun passed over the top of the island. Sunset is one of my favorite times and it is also the time that I reflect the most. I was listening to one of my favorite songs on the radio—the theme from the television show "The Greatest American Hero"—while I was making tea. I never used to drink coffee or tea but when I ran out of hot chocolate I had to have something during my cold nights at sea. Since that time I acquired a taste for it and yes, Mom, I still slurp when I drink. As I sat in the cockpit watching the sun set over the horizon I wondered what things would be like when I returned home.

I left Smugglers Cove the next day at noon and sailed to the end of Anacorpa Island. I would have liked to land and see the park there, but I needed to get back to be ready when Barbara would arrive. I turned the wheel to the east and sailed toward Santa Barbara. By six in the evening I was somewhere off of Santa Barbara. It was hard to tell where I was with the thick fog that Southern California is famous for during the summer months. Through some miracle my navigation was once again accurate and I dropped the hook right where I wanted to be at seven-thirty at night. I decided to take in a movie after I called Barbara to see what time I should meet her at the airport.

The next morning found me up at nine-thirty in the morning. Earlier than I thought I would be considering I had been up so late the night before. I bought provisions including Kool-Aid. It had been a while since I had had any. I caught a bus to the airport and splurged by having lunch at the airport. While there I ran into Dan, who crewed on a racing sloop that came into port while I was there. It was good to see Barbara coming down the stairs of the plane. After retrieving her luggage we were off to the marina.

I made dinner at anchorage and we planned the coming days'

activities. We spent a lazy morning relaxing and finally left the anchorage under sail for Arch Rocks off Santa Cruz Island. When we arrived at Arch Rocks it was time for a nap in the sunshine. We rowed ashore to explore the island and do some shell collecting. I had persuaded Barbara to help me sail back north and we decided to not waste any time on our beat back up the coast. By early evening we set a course for Point Conception, hoping to round it by daybreak. I let Barbara take the wheel and snuggled down in my berth. What a luxury not having to be a slave to the wheel.

I could see that my patience had grown a tremendous amount since I began this trip. In the past I would have complained if the crew did not take equal watches with me. Now I was grateful for any amount of time that I could be away from the demands of being a one-man crew.

Afternoons are a bad time to round a point because the wind and seas are generally at their peak then. After several tries we managed to round one of the nastiest points on the Pacific Coast. When Barbara arrived she told me stories she had heard of the problems other boats encountered trying to beat up the coast past this point. I was apprehensive about getting around Point Conception without a challenge. I had turned on the marine weather station and they were stating that the sea conditions at Point Conception were two-feet seas. We get quite a laugh about that because the fathometer is registering two fathoms from the trough to the crest. If my math is correct that is twelve feet. Every once in a while we saw a larger than normal wave come our way. Sometimes they would break just before broaching us or they would crash on top of us, soaking what few dry clothes we had. Barbara would kid me saying that must have been a three-foot wave. I was delighted to see Barbara's excitement as she marveled at all the marine life we saw. How great it was to share this joy with someone else. There was a sadness I felt because in spite of all of the beautiful things I had seen I had had no one to share it with.

The charts that I had for this trip had been very accurate until

I entered Southern California waters. Then they were almost no use at all. There were things in the water like oil rigs that were not on the charts, and there were other things listed on the charts that were no longer there. As evening was approaching, we wondered if we would be able to find San Luis Obispo or not. Then just as we were ready to head back out to sea away from the dangers of the lee shore I spotted a boat anchored. As I got closer it looked like a familiar boat. There were sleeping bags over the boom and other assorted articles of clothing on the lifelines. The boat was none other than the *La Paloma*. Rick and his wife and their twin two-year-old boys were cruising down the coast. It seemed strange but I kept running into the same people on this cruise. People making a passage down the coast will most likely keep running into each other on their trip. I first met Rick in Eureka, California. Next he showed up in Sausalito, and now here in San Luis Obispo.

I cannot describe how nice it was to be able to spend time in a calm anchorage. This was the first time in sixteen days when I was not rocking from side to side like a wild carnival ride. I did not have to hold on to something to keep from being thrown from my berth while I slept. We had a nice hot dinner and then shared a bottle of wine with Rick and his wife. There was even entertainment this evening. On shore we could see a blazing beach fire and the sounds of a party in full swing. I have to say that without a doubt, they had the worst band playing I had ever heard. After the bottle was empty Rick proceeded to write a note to put in the bottle that was just unbelievable. He wrote something about being a white slave en route to Iran but that it was okay because she was really a CIA agent sent to assassinate Ayatollah Khomeini. He then put the note in the bottle and tossed it over the side. I thought this was kind of bizarre but just think of the reaction of the person who would find this message in the bottle. The weather was so nice and the company was so good that our overnight stay turned into three blissful days protected from the headwinds and sloppy seas I had come to accept as normal.

With Barbara being on vacation we were on a time schedule to reach San Francisco. We had spent more time than we should have here so by one-thirty in the afternoon we motor sailed towards Monterey. Other than the cold at night the conditions were not very bad. The main concern while on watch seemed to be keeping warm. Barbara relieved me at the wheel after midnight as we passed Point Pedros Blancos, and I got some shut-eye. After a couple of hours Barbara awakened me to check where we were. The sight that greeted my eyes when I came out of the hatch will brighten my spirit whenever I think of it. There stood Barbara. She had taken her teeth out and was smoking one of those long black cigarettes. She had yellow foul-weather gear on with a Nor'wester cap that was tied on with a beach towel. She had another beach towel wrapped around her face so only her eyes and cigarette were uncovered. The outfit was topped off with sneakers and my ski gloves. I could not believe what I was seeing. I gave her the compass course heading and retreated to my cabin wondering if I had really seen what I thought I had. By four-thirty the next afternoon we were tied to the dock at Monterey.

The greatest thing about being at a marina is the hot showers! You end up staying until there is no more hot water, you run out of quarters, or you turn into a prune. The next thing on our agenda was to satisfy our craving for junk food. We made a trip to McDonald's for a Big Mac attack.

The next day we went through the stores on the waterfront enjoying all the paintings and curios in the shops. A quick stop for supplies and we were off to Santa Cruz, which was only a five-hour sail away. When we reached Santa Cruz we only stayed long enough for a Coke at the yacht club and then off again toward San Francisco. Our next stop on this leg of the journey would be Half Moon Bay, necessitated by the fact that we were nearly out of fuel. After filling the fuel tanks we discover that there were three gallons of fuel left. No sense taking chances. We spent just two hours in port. Long enough to eat at a restaurant and fill the fuel tanks. We were off once again for San Francisco Bay and my home away from home, Sausalito.

We left Half Moon Bay at one in the afternoon for what promised to be the fastest run of the trip. Just north of Half Moon Bay, I saw the largest sea lion I had ever seen. I was wearing my contacts so I could see real well. When I have my glasses on I can barely see past the end of the boat, but with my contacts in I can see a flea on a dog. I told Barbara to look at that huge sea lion and Barbara said, "Oh, that's just a rock." Well as soon as she said that the rock scratched its ear—which settled that.

We reached the outer buoy to San Francisco Bay in just under four hours. Sometimes we were sailing at nine knots. Just before we reached the bridge the steering cable broke and I went berserk, calling *Mary* every name I could think of. The wind was so strong I had to drop the main and steer with the emergency tiller one more time. Sailing with just the jib we were still making six knots as we passed under the Golden Gate Bridge. I told Barbara that as soon as we were past the slot towards Richardson Bay we would be in a different world, and sure enough, we were. The clothes started coming off, the cold wind was replaced by a warm sun and calm waters. We dropped the hook, glad to be out of the conditions we faced offshore.

Over the next few days I showed Barbara the sights and introduced her to some of the nice people I had met at the Sausalito cruising club. Howard and Barbara Mackey took us to Marine World with them. On Sunday Barbara and I walked to church. Sausalito is built on a mountain except for the downtown area, which is a waterfront. That means that we would have to climb a hill to go to church. And was it ever a hill. I could not believe it. It was a little more work than I cared to do again.

23.

ALONE AGAIN

I WAS NOW broke so I got a five-hundred dollar cash advance from one of the banks in town. I had spent more money in the last five days than I had the previous month. More sightseeing and eating out and it was now time for Barbara to go back home. A girl who lived near the marina had been very friendly to me, so I would see if she would like to go to a movie with me tonight after I take Barbara to the airport. As I dropped Barbara off at the airport emptiness filled her place. I did not want to be alone tonight so I went to see if the girl I met would like to see a movie. I had talked with her on several occasions in the camping area near the anchorage. She had been encouraging me earlier and then I found out that she was living with a guy there. I felt like such a fool. I do not think I will ever learn. Every time I pick a girl who looks innocent I get burned. I should try a different type of girl or give up altogether. The latter probably be the best course of action.

I went to the theater alone and saw *Raiders of the Lost Ark* for a second time. As I returned to the boat I was perplexed about my future. I had a broken engine and time running out for me to make it home for my ten-year high school reunion.

The events of the past two weeks had flown by as if I had been watching a television program. My hope of sailing home started to die when another mechanic looked at the engine on *Mary*. The mechanic said that the problem with the engine was major so I checked around to see how much it would cost to ship *Mary* home. I was shocked to find out that it would cost twelve hundred dollars. The mechanic said that the problem with the engine was a bad valve. I figured I did not have anything to lose so I decided to pull the head off the engine myself and see if I could fix it. The head turned out to have a bad exhaust valve and I ended up playing the waiting game only to find out one week later that the shop ordered the wrong valve and that the one that I needed was already in stock. Time was starting to turn into an enemy. I was starting to feel the pressure on my life once more. I realized that most of the pressures in my life I imposed on myself.

I had the same dream several nights in a row now, which made me feel very uneasy. I usually never remember my dreams. On the rare occasion that I can remember a dream it has always been about future events that always seem to come true. In this dream I was trying to fight my way off a lee shore with rocks threatening to crush *Mary*. As in previous dreams, it ended with me in a precarious place. I wondered about my destiny and if I had the power to change what happens. Did the dream ending as it did mean that I have the power to change the outcome? While waiting for parts I had the opportunity to see Tristan Jones again and buy his book *Adrift*, which he autographed for me. You can learn a lot about a person through his writing. The next morning I rowed ashore to pick up David and Ann to have breakfast aboard *Mary*.

The next day was an ambitious one for me. I did all the cleaning and the repair work, and except for the engine the boat was ready for sea. *Mary* had been good to me. What about the future though? The Mackeys, whom I met at the Sausalito cruising club, had been so nice to me the past few weeks. Howard had taken me places to pick up parts and supplies and I decided to let him sail with me up the coast if all went well.

The next several days were ones of relaxing with friends and resting. Lee and I played chess and we all shared meals on each other's boats. Sometimes we just walked up to town and took in all the sites. I called home and got to talk to everyone. It was so great to be able to hear from those I love. Howard and I looked at the Coronado thirty-two today and I was impressed. Maybe someday I will get a boat with better accommodations. Back at the anchorage everyone visited until after midnight. The last few days had been disappointment on top of disappointment for me and sometimes I wondered if God was trying to break me. I could not get the mast lights working and after trying for three days, I figured what was the use and started feeling sorry for myself, believing everything was against me. The day finally arrived when the head was ready to put back on the engine. As most times when I work on *Mary*, I had to persuade her by screaming, fighting, and swearing until she gave in and worked. I was ready to tackle the long beat up the coast, or at least I thought I was.

24.

THE JOURNEY ENDS

HOWARD AND I left port on August 1, and were in for a fight from the start. The tide was flooding in so our speed was really slow. The engine exhaust came off even before we got to the Golden Gate Bridge. After I repaired it we were on our way again. The exhaust fumes that filled the boat made it unbearable below decks. Near Point Reyes we were met by six- to eight-foot seas that were really close together. We just could not make any headway so after an hour of watching the same rocks offshore I talked it over with Howard and we decided that a wise thing to do would be to go back and try again. I had never felt so beaten or defeated, but I used good judgment in making the decision. I believed that whether I sailed *Mary* home or had her trailered home would determine what direction my life would take. There is no way to describe how I felt in my spirit. On top of everything else I was getting the worst headache of my life. I knew it was carbon monoxide poisoning from the engine exhaust. I just felt like giving up. Once we were back at Sausalito and Howard went home I took some Percodan and called it a night. Maybe things would look better tomorrow.

The next day *Mary* was loaded on a trailer to be shipped home. As I saw her leave I started to cry like a baby. I feel as if I had let her down and that I was a failure. I remembered all that we had been through and that she had never let me down, but I had let her down. This was the first time in my life that I did not finish something that I started. So here I was waiting to see if I could catch the next plane home. The air traffic controllers just went out on strike. I could not bring myself to pay what they want for a room so I and hundreds of other stranded travelers are walking about the airport. Have you ever noticed that all the benches at the airport have arm rests on them so you cannot lie down? People were sleeping on the floor in their sleeping bags waiting for flights to leave. As I thought back and reflected on the past few months I saw advantages to traveling by *Mary* that I did not see before. When you are sailing you have everything with you. You are like an island, self-sufficient and independent. The drawbacks are also evident—the storms I encountered and the time it took me to get someplace. I would cover more distance in ten minutes by air than I could sail in a day. They say that half the fun of being someplace is in getting there, or so I have been told. That might be open to debate. When things went wrong I would scream at *Mary* and tell her I hated her, but I did not realize until this moment that I also loved her.

So once again, a chapter in my life was ending and a different type of adventure awaited. The process of beginning and ending had started again. I do not mind telling you that the future was far more frightening than any storm that raged around me during this voyage. I was so uncertain of what awaited me when I got home, and I guess I was also nervous. You see I have never really liked myself very much. When I look in the mirror I see all the flaws of the person who is looking at me. During the six months I had been on this adventure I had the privilege of meeting many exceptional people. While on this voyage, though, I met someone I never expected to meet and in spite of all of his shortcomings and failures I saw beyond them and realized that he is okay. He is not the person that he will become, but he continues to learn and to grow. **The person I met on this trip was me!**

PHOTOS AND MAPS

Gary Dickinson in front of *Mary*—launching day.

Mary launched.

Forward Cabin of *Mary*.

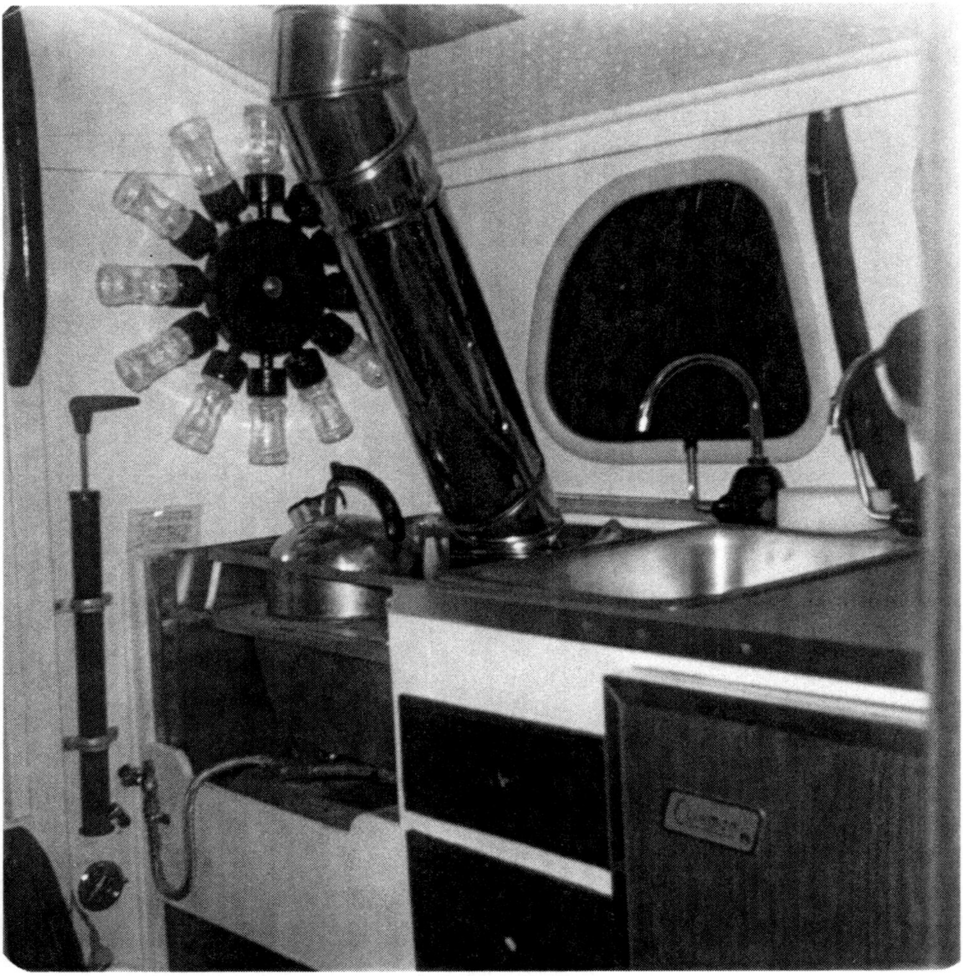

Galley of *Mary*.

Aft Cabin of *Mary*.

Curt and I starting voyage.

Mary anchored at Angel Island.

Curt Nielsen at the wheel.

Dave Rockwood with Mike and Joan Wey on Angel Island.

(*Mary*) self-steering off the southern California coast.

These are some of the Incidence that took place during the voyage.

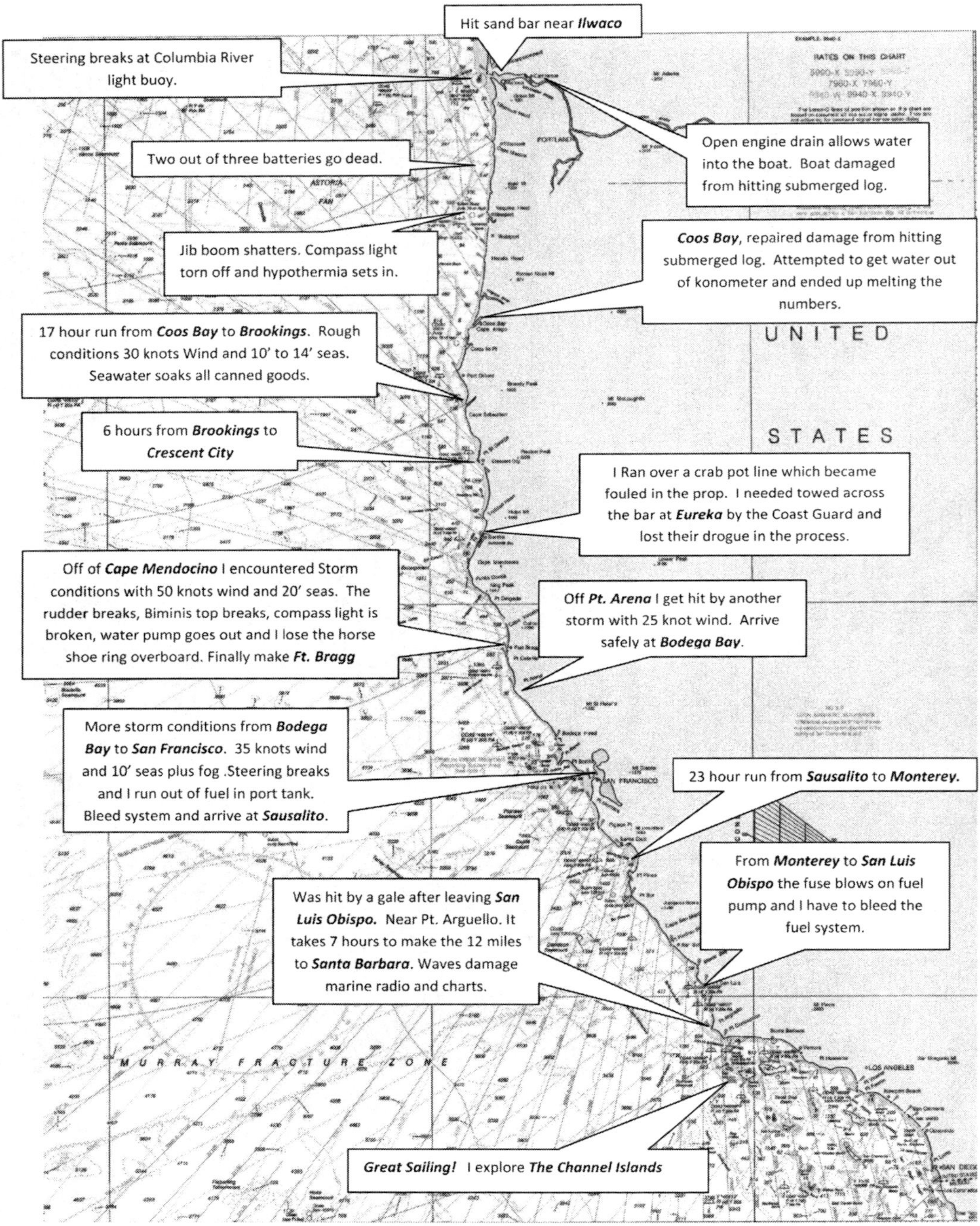

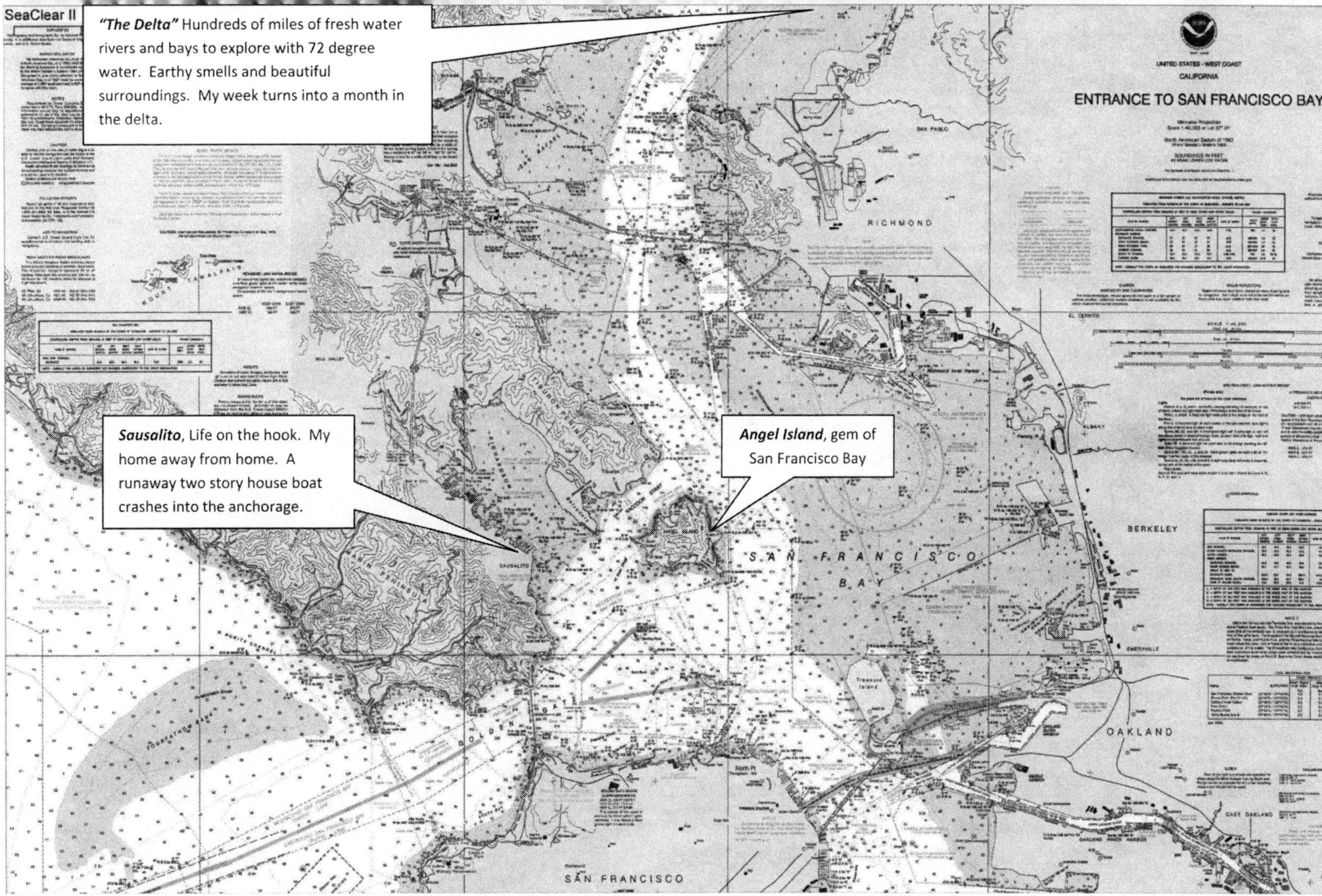
SeaClear II
"The Delta" Hundreds of miles of fresh water rivers and bays to explore with 72 degree water. Earthy smells and beautiful surroundings. My week turns into a month in the delta.
UNITED STATES - WEST COAST
CALIFORNIA
ENTRANCE TO SAN FRANCISCO BAY
RICHMOND
Sausalito, Life on the hook. My home away from home. A runaway two story house boat crashes into the anchorage.
Angel Island, gem of San Francisco Bay
SAN FRANCISCO BAY
BERKELEY
OAKLAND
SAN FRANCISCO

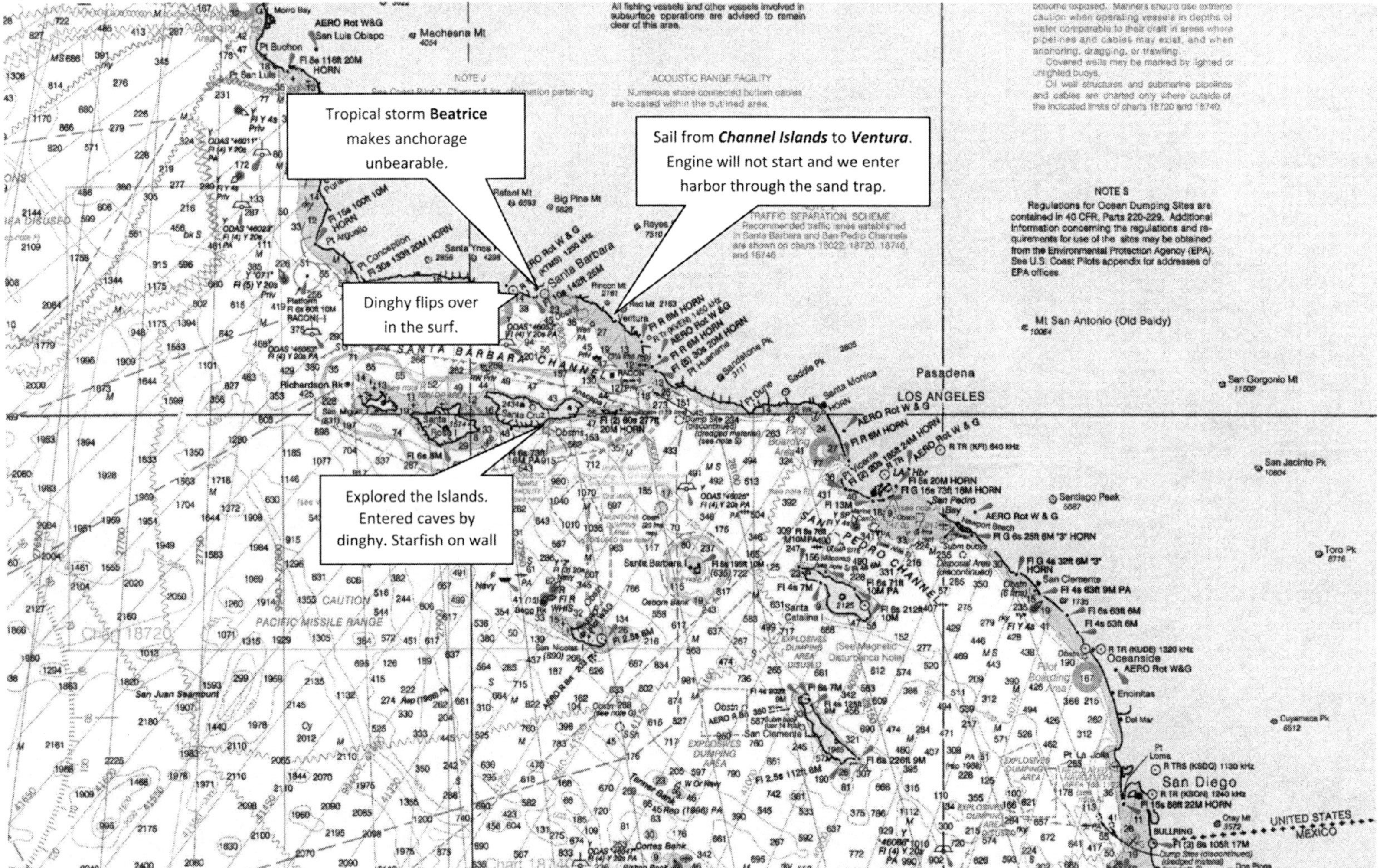
Tropical storm **Beatrice** makes anchorage unbearable.
Sail from ***Channel Islands*** to ***Ventura***. Engine will not start and we enter harbor through the sand trap.
Dinghy flips over in the surf.
Explored the Islands. Entered caves by dinghy. Starfish on wall
SANTA BARBARA CHANNEL
SAN PEDRO CHANNEL
Santa Barbara
Ventura
LOS ANGELES
Pasadena
San Diego
Oceanside
San Clemente
Santa Catalina I
Mt San Antonio (Old Baldy)
UNITED STATES
MEXICO
PACIFIC MISSILE RANGE
NOTE S
Regulations for Ocean Dumping Sites are contained in 40 CFR, Parts 220-229. Additional information concerning the regulations and requirements for use of the sites may be obtained from the Environmental Protection Agency (EPA). See U.S. Coast Pilots appendix for addresses of EPA offices.
All fishing vessels and other vessels involved in subsurface operations are advised to remain clear of this area.

Printed in the United States
122812LV00003B/104/P